‖‖ ‖ ‖‖‖‖‖‖‖‖‖‖‖ ‖ ‖‖‖‖‖‖‖‖ ‖‖‖‖‖‖ ‖‖

☑ **KU-741-282**

REPORT OF A WORKING PARTY ON THE TEACHING OF MEDICAL ETHICS

Chairman:– Sir Desmond Pond

Edited by Kenneth M Boyd
Scottish Director, Institute of Medical Ethics

THE BRITISH SCHOOL OF OSTEOPATHY
1-4 SUFFOLK ST., LONDON. SW1Y 4HG
TEL. 01 · 930 9254-8

IME Publications Ltd.
London 1987

IME Publications Ltd,
151 Great Portland Street,
London W1N 5PB

© *Institute of Medical Ethics, 1987*

All rights are reserved. No part of this publication may be reproduced, stored in a retrieval system, or transmitted, in any form or by an means, electronic, mechanical, photocopying, recording, or otherwise, without the prior permission of

IME Publications Ltd

ISBN 1-870550-00-5

Printed in Great Britain by
Inprint of Luton Ltd,
Luton, Bedfordshire

On Medical Ethics

'One is ethical — I mean, for heaven's sake — is one not?'

A DOCTOR

'These ethical issues are terribly important, and clearly your view on them is as good as mine and mine's as good as yours, and I have more experience...'

A MEDICAL TEACHER TO MEDICAL STUDENTS

'Does ethics lead doctors to better decisions as a result of thinking? Are they "better" because they approximate more closely to "right answers", or because they are more consistent with each other? Or could asking doctors to think explicitly and systematically about ethics actually lead them, in some cases, to take worse decisions than those based on intuition and experience?'

A PHILOSOPHER

Members of the working party

Sir Desmond Pond, MA, MD, FRCP, FRCPsych, (Chairman)
Chief Scientist, DHSS, 1982-85.

Professor Sir Douglas Black, MD, FRCP
President, Institute of Medical Ethics

Professor Gerald Dworkin, LLB
Professor of Law, University of Southampton

Jonathan Glover, MA, DPhil
Fellow and tutor in Philosophy, New College, Oxford

Evelyn Hide, MA, SRN, SCM, RNT, DipEd
Lecturer, St Bartholomew's School of Nursing, London

Roger Higgs, MA, MB, MRCP
Director of General Practice Studies, King's College, London

Professor Bryan Jennett, MD, FRCS
Dean, Faculty of Medicine, University of Glasgow

Professor Desmond Laurence, MD, FRCP
Professor of Pharmacology and Therapeutics, University College, London

Marshall Marinker, MB, BS, FRCGP
Director, MSD Foundation, London.

Gordon Marsh, MA, FHA
Deputy Health Service Commissioner, but serving in his personal capacity.

Prebendary Edward Shotter, BA
Director, Institute of Medical Ethics, *ex officio.*

Ann Thomson, BA, SRN, SCM, MTD
Lecturer, Department of Nursing, University of Manchester

Professor Keith Ward, MA BLitt
Professor of Moral and Social Theology, King's College, London.

Richard West, MD, FRCP, DCH, DObstRCOG
Dean, St George's Hospital Medical School, London.

RESEARCH TEAM

Kenneth M Boyd, MA, BD, PhD, (Secretary)
Scottish Director, Institute of Medical Ethics

Brendan Callaghan SJ, MA, MPhil, MTh
Principal, Heythrop College, University of London.

Raanan Gillon, BA, MB, BS, MRCP
Editor, *Journal of Medical Ethics*

Mary Lobjoit, MB, ChB
Co-ordinating Secretary, Manchester Medical Group.

Richard Nicholson, MA, BM, DCH
Editor, *IME Bulletin.*

PREFACE

The purpose of this Preface is to commend this Report to the consideration of those responsible for the ordering of the curriculum, many of whom have contributed important information to the deliberations of the Working Party. My purpose is not, however, to summarise the message of the Report, which speaks for itself.

But I do have another and more immediate purpose, which is to pay tribute to our Chairman, Sir Desmond Pond, who contributed so much of enthusiasm, critical thought, and exquisite balance to an important and difficult enterprise. Sir Desmond was distinguished in many other ways, and diverse walks of life; but in a sense this Report represents a crowning achievement, for in spite of advancing illness he was able to see it through to virtual completion — 'continuing the same until it was thoroughly finished'. It is the hope and expectation of all his colleagues on the Working Party that this Report will become widely known and much referred to as 'The Pond Report'.

Sir Douglas Black

ACKNOWLEDGEMENTS

The Institute of Medical Ethics is greatly indebted to the trustees of the Nuffield Foundation, not only for generously funding the study on which this book is based, but also for making the splendid facilities of Nuffield Lodge available for meetings of the Working Party. The Institute is particularly grateful to the Director of the Foundation and to its staff for their courtesy and helpfulness. The Institute is indebted also to all those medical Deans, teachers and students who provided so much information and especially to the members of the Working Party, who gave generously of their time and accumulated wisdom. For assistance in organising the study and preparing the report, the Institute wishes to thank Mrs M Price, Mrs L M McDiarmid, Mr C R Dinnis and Miss T Moncreiff.

CONTENTS

CHAPTER ONE: WHAT IS MEDICAL ETHICS AND CAN IT BE TAUGHT?

CHAPTER TWO: THE SCOPE OF MEDICAL ETHICS

CHAPTER THREE: EXISTING ARRANGEMENTS FOR MEDICAL ETHICS TEACHING

CHAPTER FOUR: RECOMMENDATIONS

INTRODUCTION

In 1984, with encouragement from the General Medical Council and a grant from the Nuffield Foundation, the Institute of Medical Ethics convened a Working Party to study the teaching of medical ethics in British medical schools. The Working Party was asked to express and illustrate its understanding of 'medical ethics teaching' and to identify existing teaching arrangements. It was asked further, to discuss alternative teaching options, academic standards and possible pitfalls, and to make recommendations. This book is the result of its work.

The Working Party included teachers from various medical specialities, the Deans of two medical schools, representatives of professions, including nursing, associated with medicine, and teachers of law, philosophy and theology. It was chaired, with skill, courtesy and good humour, by Sir Desmond Pond, formerly Professor of Psychiatry at the London Hospital Medical College and, in 1984, Chief Scientist at the DHSS. The members of the Working Party not only came from different disciplines, but held a wide variety of different opinions on medical ethics and how it should be taught. It was no small tribute to Sir Desmond Pond that the Working Party eventually reached a degree of consensus on these subjects. His death, on the 29th of June 1986, greatly saddened the members of the Working Party and everyone associated with the work of the Institute.

Not long before his death, Sir Desmond annotated and approved the final draft of the Working Party's report, which the other members also approved some days later and which is found in the following pages.

KMB

CHAPTER ONE

What is medical ethics and can it be taught?

The initial question

1.1 It is often claimed that medical ethics cannot be taught. Competence and compassion, it is argued, are acquired by experience or 'osmosis', while the moral views of individuals differ and ultimately are a personal matter. Such arguments create an understandable suspicion that 'medical ethics teaching' may be a matter either of abstract theorising or of moral indoctrination, neither of which should have a place in medical education.

1.2 But are moral choices entirely a matter for the individual doctor, and is there no place in medical education for explicit teaching about the ethics of medical practice? On many medico-moral questions, it might be pointed out, the medical profession itself has a corporate view, which it does not hesitate to commend to its members. In an increasing number of medical schools, moreover, the need for medical ethics teaching is now acknowledged, not least because of its practical relevance to present-day problems.

1.3 Present-day moral problems in medical practice, it may be agreed, provide the context in which the question of teaching medical ethics should be addressed. In this context, it can be argued, **the first and most relevant question is not whether a new subject should be added to the curriculum, but how medical ethics, which always has been central to medical practice, should be understood, and how that understanding should be expressed in medical education.** In addressing this question, it may be helpful, at the outset, to distinguish between two different senses in which 'medical ethics' is commonly used.*

Two meanings of 'medical ethics'

1.4 'Medical ethics', traditionally, has referred to the standards of professional competence and conduct which the medical profession expects of its members. Medical ethics in this sense

---

* The words 'ethical' (derived from Greek) and 'moral' (derived from Latin) mean much the same. 'Ethics' is often preferred when talking about the study of ethical or moral questions, or when referring to professed moral standards. 'Morals' also may be used in this way, but more commonly refers to actual conduct. One should not read too much significance into the distinction however. In this report, it is hoped, the meaning may be apparent from the context.

embraces formal and informal codes of practice, matters of etiquette and medical communication, and the maintenance of minimum standards, which the profession seeks to convert into standards of excellence. Because patients need to trust the competence and integrity of doctors, it has been widely accepted that medical ethics in this first sense should be taught to medical students, both by example and by explicit reference to existing codes and guidelines.

1.5 'Medical ethics' also is used, increasingly, in a second sense. This refers to the study of ethical or moral **problems** raised by the practice of medicine. These problems may take the form of acute 'moral dilemmas', but equally may be concerned with the moral assumptions underlying everyday decisions about what doctors ought to do or say. Among the reasons why these are problems, is that normally they cannot be resolved simply by appealing to professional codes, or to science, religion, the law or even common sense. These problems often arise, indeed, when there is a conflict between different principles embodied in accepted codes, or when principles previously accepted begin to be questioned, or are understood imperfectly or even misrepresented.

1.6 'Medical ethics' in this second sense has attracted greater attention in recent decades as a result of medico-moral dilemmas posed by scientific and technical progress. But essentially it is nothing new. Doctors and others, each with different moral viewpoints, have always engaged in informal rational argument about medical ethics – argument, that is, in which reasons for and against different moral positions have been defended and criticised. Systematic argument about ethical questions, moreover, has been the traditional concern of disciplines such as moral philosophy and moral theology, each often referred to as 'ethics'. These disciplines are long-established, not only in general University education, but also in the education of a number of other professions.

Two potential benefits

1.7 Whether undertaken systematically or informally, rational argument about ethical questions offers at least two potential benefits to those who engage in it. First, it can contribute to greater intellectual awareness of the kind of reasoning being used in one's own and others' moral thinking. With this in mind, teaching about medical ethics in this second sense may be compared to teaching about scientific method – as opposed to teaching medicine by rote learning. Second, rational argument about ethical questions can contribute to an extension of understanding and sympathy. Having to take seriously the moral arguments of others, that is, can lead to the discovery that those with whom one disagrees, even on fairly fundamental matters, are neither wicked nor stupid – but have moral positions of their own which, like one's own, can be both defended and criticised.

1.8 These potential benefits have particular relevance to present-day moral problems in medical practice. Many of these problems have arisen not only as a result of scientific and technical progress, but also because of organisational and social change. On the one hand, health services are now highly complex organisations, in which doctors are in a minority. On the other, society is now more extensively informed, particularly by the media, about the moral choices which doctors have to make – but society is far from agreed on the answers to the moral questions involved. In this context, doctors are increasingly likely to encounter others who do not share their own professional or personal moral assumptions. **Greater awareness and understanding, on the part of doctors, of their own and others' moral thinking, thus have an important part to play in facilitating better communication, not only between doctors and patients, and doctors and other health workers, but also among doctors themselves.**

1.9 How far can 'medical ethics teaching' be expected to lead to these practical benefits? Some activities which might be given this name – the 'abstract theorising' or 'moral indoctrination' already referred to – are unlikely to achieve this; and indeed any form of ethics teaching which suggests either that 'it is all too difficult', or that there are known and incontrovertible 'right answers', is likely to be counterproductive. But other activities seem more promising. The need for medical ethics teaching, acknowledged by many medical teachers, has led to a variety of initiatives; and in some medical schools a certain amount of exploratory, undogmatic, practice-oriented teaching and learning has begun to be undertaken. From what it has learned of this, the Working Party believes that the teaching of medical ethics, in the second as well as the first sense, not only is possible, but ought to be encouraged.

No specific syllabus

1.10 The Working Party believes that the teaching of medical ethics ought to be encouraged. It believes also that some ways of teaching are more appropriate than others (see chapter 4). It does not wish, however, to recommend a specific syllabus for medical ethics teaching. The main reason for this, as already mentioned, is that medical ethics should be seen, not as a new subject to be added to the curriculum, but as a vital aspect of all medical practice, the implications of which should be made explicit throughout medical education. A further reason for not recommending one specific syllabus is that the curricula of British medical schools vary considerably, particularly with reference to the integration of subjects and of pre-clinical and clinical teaching. What may be possible or desirable in one medical school may not be in another; and this will vary also in relation to the presence or absence of teaching resources in other Faculties of the local University, insofar as it is thought appropriate to involve these.

Local initiatives and review

1.11 These considerations suggest that, **at present, the teaching of medical ethics will be best encouraged by encouraging local initiatives, making use of opportunities which can be created within the resources available to each medical school.** This recommendation is made on the understanding that the need for medical ethics teaching (for the reasons outlined above) is likely to grow, as are opportunities for medical teachers to improve their skills of explicit communication with particular reference to medical ethics in the second sense. **In seeking to encourage local initiatives therefore, the Working Party envisages that experience of these, over the next five years, will provide an opportunity for reassessment of alternative teaching options at the end of this period.**

Options recommended

1.12 While envisaging reassessment at a later date, the Working Party also believes that some assessment of alternative teaching options can be made at present. Chapter 3 of this Report records the Working Party's findings concerning existing arrangements for the teaching of medical ethics in British medical schools. This chapter includes also some account of the views of medical teachers and medical students on the teaching of medical ethics. In Chapter 4, with these findings in view, **the Working Party recommends a number of particular teaching options which might be adapted to local circumstances, together with others which it might seem advisable to avoid.** Chapter 4 discusses also the questions of: a) academic standards in medical ethics teaching; b) the contribution to such teaching of disciplines other than medicine; and c) the role of extra-curricular and post-graduate opportunities for the study of medical ethics. Before these matters are discussed however, Chapter 2 considers the scope of medical ethics and how this relates to medical ethics teaching.

CHAPTER TWO

The scope of medical ethics

Introduction

2.1 The last chapter stated that medical ethics is, and always has been, central to medical practice. To illustrate this, the present chapter sketches the historical background (paragraphs 2.2 and 2.3), and indicates some of the ethical issues which arise within different medical specialities, and in relation to other professions in health care (paragraphs 2.4 to 2.14). This short summary is intended not as an exhaustive account of the scope of medical ethics, but to demonstrate the range and variety of ethical issues with which teaching might be concerned. With this in mind, the chapter goes on to note some common themes and underlying conflicts among basic ethical principles (paragraphs 2.15 and 2.16) and concludes with some remarks on the scope and limits of medical ethics teaching (paragraphs 2.17 to 2.20).

Historical background

2.2 The history of medical ethics is not seen by the Working Party as a necessary ingredient of medical ethics teaching. It is referred to here, however, to illustrate the statement that medical ethics always has been central to medical practice, and to do this with particular reference to the two senses in which 'medical ethics' has come to be used. The mistaken popular belief that all doctors 'have taken the Hippocratic Oath', for example, reflects, if obscurely, the historical evidence that professional medical ethics ('medical ethics' in the first sense) has existed since Hippocratic times. In those times, historians now believe, the Oath was as much religious as professional and was 'taken' by no more than a minority of Greek physicians[1]. But some of its main concerns (in modern terms, those of education, accreditation, remuneration and the physician's skills and integrity) seem to have been central also even to the more ancient ideals of the primitive medicine man.[2] Taken up in turn by Christian and Enlightenment culture, these basic Hippocratic concerns persisted into the 19th and 20th centuries, during which they helped to shape the modern medical profession's ethical standards of organisation, competence and conduct.

2.3 Historical evidence of the study of moral problems raised by the practice of medicine ('medical ethics' in the second sense) may be less obvious. In the past, the relative ineffectiveness of medicine's armamentarium may have made it seem more relevant to be 'philosophical' about necessary evils, than to argue (in the manner of modern philosophical medical ethics) about conflicting values and principles. From classical until relatively recent times, moreover, most public argument about medico-moral questions was conducted in the language of a common religious culture, subject to ecclesiastical authority. As the sea of faith ebbed however, many now-familiar medico-moral problems were uncovered. Initially, in the 18th and 19th centuries, debate in medical ethics in the second sense focused upon what should constitute medical ethics in the first sense – questions about the physician's moral character and relationships with patients, colleagues, science and the state.[3] Subsequently, during the 19th and 20th centuries, debate began to focus also on such questions as medical experiments with animals and humans, euthanasia, and abortion[4] – the last two in particular illustrating that previously accepted principles (of the Hippocratic Oath) had begun to be questioned. During the second half of the 20th century, when the full range and variety of ethical questions raised by medical practice began to become apparent, even more fundamental Hippocratic principles were seen, on occasion, to be in conflict with other moral principles which were no less important. A new respect for the autonomy of the individual, for example, might conflict with the doctor's duty, above all to avoid harm (or what the doctor judged to be harm) to the individual patient. Or again, a new awareness of the obligation to allocate scarce resources fairly might conflict with the doctor's traditional duty to give priority to the interest of his individual patient.

Medicine and Surgery

2.4 Conflicts of this kind may be seen in a variety of medical specialties today. But beginning with the major disciplines of Medicine and Surgery, an additional reason for growing interest in ethical issues may be immediately apparent. The advent of what is termed 'High Technology Medicine' has made it difficult to avoid a large number of medico-moral questions – about, for example, prolonging life, defining death, withdrawing life-support, preserving dignity, obtaining consent, resuscitation, euthanasia, 'the living will', 'medical heroics', medical priorities and responsibility for decision-making.

These are topical questions, of interest to medical students, to doctors in many specialities, to nurses and other health workers, and to the public. As such, they provide a focus for teaching medical ethics in both the second and first senses – teaching, that is, which explores conflicts in practice and in principle, and is concerned also with questions about medical communication with other professions, patients and the public.

2.5 Moral conflicts and matters of medical communication arise not only in connection with 'High Technology Medicine', but also elsewhere in Medicine and Surgery. In Therapeutics and Clinical Pharmacology, to take only one example, the ethical aspects of prescribing and administering drugs include not only the maintenance of standards of care and competence, but also moral problems about what patients and doctors expect from medicine: the same prescription, on occasion, may be seen by the patient as a cure for living and by the doctor as a means of getting rid of a difficult patient. Such questions arise from the earliest stages of medical practice, and even for medical students, for whom relationships between doctors and the pharmaceutical industry already may cause moral problems.

General Practice

2.6 General Practice raises questions both about confidence and confidentiality and about intimacy and intrusiveness in the doctor-patient relationship. Some ethical issues here again are topical, for example those concerning autonomy and consent in the case of teenage patients requesting contraceptive advice or abortion. But equally important moral questions arise in decisions about whether or not to persuade elderly patients to enter long-term care. More generally, the GP's role as gatekeeper of the health care system frequently involves making moral and economic as well as strictly medical judgements. As a generalist, responsible for a population as well as the individual patient, the GP is required to take many decisions at or near the limits of his own competence. These include estimates of probability and risk in the diagnosis of early disease across the whole spectrum of specialties, together with the crucial question of whether or not to refer. They include also, decisions related to the GP's role in the relief of social need, with reference to matters such as housing and social benefits. Further questions of competence arise again in relation to the 'treatment' of family or social problems which may be seen as contributing to the complaint of the presenting patient.

Obstetrics and Gynaecology

2.7 Ethical issues in Obstetrics and Gynaecology are among those best known to the public. They include the moral problems of contraception, sterilisation and therapeutic abortion, and also,

7

more recently, those of artificial insemination, *in vitro* fertilisation and research on embryos. Religious and cultural questions may be prominent in relation to these issues, and also to those of antenatal diagnosis, antenatal care generally, and choice in child-birth. Stillbirth and the care of grieving patients and staff raise further ethical issues. Many medico-moral aspects of Obstetrics and Gynaecology are of concern also to General Practice and to other specialities. Clinical Genetics, for example, has an interest in antenatal diagnosis, genetic counselling and the prevention of inherited disease and mental retardation or handicap. The last, including ethical questions about the sterilisation of mentally handicapped individuals, is of interest also to Psychiatry and Paediatrics. A variety of ethical issues involving different specialities arise, too, in connection with sexually transmitted diseases.

Child Health and Paediatrics

2.8 In Child Health and Paediatrics many problems of medical ethics become more complicated because the autonomy of the child varies with age and stage of development. The question of parental rights over the child is involved also and it may be particularly difficult for the doctor to assess what is in the child's best interests. In neonatal paediatrics, the management of major handicap poses major ethical problems, raised acutely but not resolved by the case of Dr Arthur. The continuing management of handicapped children involves further ethical problems about what level of care is appropriate. Other ethical issues of concern to Paediatrics (in addition to those mentioned in the two preceding paragraphs) include questions about children as potential organ donors for other members of their family, questions of risk and consent in research involving children, questions about immunization, and the problem of child abuse.

Psychiatry

2.9 In Psychiatry also, many medico-moral problems are further complicated by the patient's condition. Because psychiatric illness may impair judgement, acute conflicts may be created here between the patient's autonomy and the therapist's judgement about what is in the patient's best interests. Questions involved include the difficulty of assessing the patient's dangerousness to himself or others, the justification of compulsory detention or treatment, the ethics of behaviour modification, the prevention of suicide and the management of depression. Other ethical issues in Psychiatry range from those of the use of surrogates in sexual therapy, to those of withholding treatment in severe senile dementia. In Psychiatry also, the ethical problems of communication with patients' families are raised acutely.

Geriatric Medicine and Care of the Elderly

2.10 Ethical issues in Geriatric Medicine and Care of the Elderly are particularly important because the present generation of medical students will be serving the needs of an ageing population. Problems involved in this area include not only those related to autonomy (as exemplified above with reference to General Practice), but also those of determining the goals and limits of care and treatment. In this context, questions about 'euthanasia' are sometimes raised with reference to demented elderly patients. These questions however may be inappropriate, betraying more about the feelings of the onlooker than those of the patient. As with related questions in the area of Terminal Care, the different meanings of 'euthanasia' (from the literal 'a good death' or 'dying well' to more radical demands for assisted suicide or even homicide) require careful examination. So too do the range of practical alternatives available. Geriatric Medicine, again, has particular responsibility for teaching the professional ethics of care and competence in diagnosis and treatment of the elderly, as well as for co-operation with other health professions and patients' families in maintaining autonomy and dignity both in hospital and in the community.

Community Medicine and Forensic Medicine

2.11 Many of the ethical issues discussed above are of concern also to Community, Social or Preventive Medicine, and to the area of Behavioural Sciences. Social, environmental and economic questions may be involved in many ethical issues, while conflicts of loyalty may arise in the areas of Occupational Health and of the planning and organisation of health care and health promotion. Problems of medical ethics, however, are not reducible to the terms of the disciplines associated with Community Medicine, nor indeed to those of Forensic or Legal Medicine, which in the past often has taken responsibility for teaching 'medical ethics'. While knowledge of Legal Medicine is essential for medical students, 'medical ethics' in the two senses understood in this Report, has both clinical and moral dimensions which go far beyond the particular and distinct concerns of both Forensic and Community Medicine.

Research

2.12 In relation to many of the disciplines discussed above, moral problems may be raised for medical students by their involvement, while still in training, either in the conduct of research projects or as the subjects of research. Ethical questions in this context may be concerned with research design, risks and benefits, informed consent, communication with patients and other health workers, and the role of research ethics committees. A particularly significant problem here may be that of the validity of consent in the context of the student/teacher relationship. In its *Recommendations on Basic Medical Education*(1980), the General Medical Council specifically states under the heading of 'Ethics', that the attention of medical students should 'be directed to the ethical responsibilities of the medical profession in clinical investigation and in research, and in the development of new therapeutic procedures'.

Nursing

2.13 Ethical questions exist not only within medical specialities but also between medicine and other associated professions. Seen from a Nursing viewpoint, for example, ethical problems not uncommonly arise in relation to the information which doctors communicate to or withhold from patients or nurses, the inclusion of patients in medical research, and medical decisions to use or withhold different kinds or treatment, particularly in the care of the elderly or terminally ill. While professional medical ethics has always been concerned with the etiquette of consultation and delegation, the growing professional awareness of Nursing and, in different contexts, the concept of the 'Health Care Team', may raise a variety of new ethical questions about medical responsibility and communication.

Management and Administration

2.14 Similar problems to the above may be found in doctors' relationships with other groups working in health care. In the particular case of Health Care Managers (who themselves may be doctors or nurses as well as administrators) the allocation of scarce resources may give rise to conflict about priorities and how the needs of different patient groups or individual patients are to be measured and weighed against others'. In relationships between clinicians and administrators moreover, there may be conflicts of loyalty where confidentiality is involved or when doctors have made mistakes in treatment, which then lead to legal proceedings.

10

Many of these problems are further complicated by the rise of consumer, pressure and representative groups of various kinds.

Common themes

2.15 Many ethical issues then, arise today, both in different medical specialities and in medicine's relationship with associated disciplines. Within this spectrum, major recurring themes include those of competence, consent, confidentiality, communication and priorities. All of these are matters with which traditional or professional medical ethics has been concerned. But all, too, may raise ethical problems in present-day medical practice. These problems, it is increasingly recognised, often reflect conflict between basic ethical principles.

Beneficence, Autonomy and Justice

2.16 To many moral philosophers, the most important of these basic ethical principles are those commonly referred to as: 1) Beneficence and Non-Maleficence; 2) Respect for Autonomy; and 3) Justice. The principle of Beneficence and Non-Maleficence is concerned with the doctor's duty where possible to do good, and always to do no harm, to those in his care. This principle is fundamental to the traditional ethics of the medical profession, its negative or minimal (Non-Maleficence) form being the familiar *primum non nocere* (above all, do no harm). In the context of present-day medical practice however, the primacy of this first principle may be challenged by the second or the third. The second principle, that of Respect for Autonomy, is concerned with the duty to respect, not obstruct and wherever possible facilitate the freedom of the individual (patient, but also doctor) to make responsible choices about his own life. This second principle recognises that the individual's actual autonomy may be restricted by internal or external constraints, but seeks to maximise whatever potential exists. Among the possible external constraints are the needs and wishes of other people. The principle of Justice also is concerned with these and with the duty to be as fair as possible to all concerned, both in the distribution of resources and in respecting their rights. This third principle requires that the demands of Beneficence and Autonomy in the case of one individual should be weighed against similar requirements in the case of others. In practice, of course, this may be extremely difficult to do, and the difficulty is compounded when the demands of Beneficence and Autonomy in any one case themselves conflict. A further aspect of the principle of Justice thus is not only that justice should be done, but that it should be seen and agreed to have been done: the third principle, in other words, is concerned not only with the question of what is decided, but also with that of who decides.

Medical ethics teaching

2.17 The preceding discussion, it can be argued, illustrates at least part of the scope of medical ethics teaching. The initial aims of ethics teaching are to help students develop both an awareness of where and what the ethical problems are, and an intellectual framework within which these problems can be examined. The particular elements of a framework mentioned in the previous paragraph are only some among others which might have been suggested. What matters at this initial stage is that students should be alerted to the range and variety of medico-moral problems, and encouraged to think for themselves about how these problems relate to one another, to more general ethical issues, and to the student's own attitudes, beliefs and values.

A body of knowledge

2.18 The scope of medical ethics teaching is not limited to this, however. Medical education introduces students to an understanding of health and sickness related to a range and variety of complex interactions, involving molecules, cells, tissues, organs, systems, individuals and social groups. At each of these levels of organisation, study of a body of knowledge is required, the precision of that knowledge differing at different levels, or according to what can be known about interaction between these levels. The study of medical ethics is not dissimilar to this. The relevant body of knowledge includes not only the codes and standards of professional medical ethics, but also the systematic analysis of moral arguments undertaken by ethics in general. Because few if any moral conclusions are ultimately incontestable (most being, in practice, provisional), study of this body of knowledge does not necessarily lead to answers upon which all informed disputants would agree. The purpose of study, rather, is to help the student become aware that even the most complex moral problems can be analysed in a systematic, critical and disciplined manner. These problems are neither 'too personal' nor 'too difficult' to be discussed rationally with other people and their moral dimensions mapped out in some generally agreed way.

The clinical context

2.19 In basic medical education, pressures on the curriculum will limit study of this body of ethical knowledge. Elective opportunities, of course, might be made available for those who wish to study ethical theory or particular ethical questions in greater detail. But for most students, the most appropriate teaching method will probably be that of classical moral enquiry – a matter of starting from everyday examples, and then asking leading questions. Such questions cannot properly be treated without a theoretical examination of the reasons for different moral views, clarification of concepts, and discussion of underlying principles and values. How far the questions lead, in any particular discussion, will depend on the context. In the context of basic medical education, the analogous place to begin is with clinical examples and histories, taking all the relevant clinical as well as ethical features fully into account. In this context moreover, full account has to be taken of the fact that basic medical education is a preparation for practice in which doctors have to make decisions. With this in mind, ethics teaching will encourage students not only to articulate the ethical and clinical features of a particular case, but also to express a clinical judgement about the most appropriate course of action. Having expressed this judgement, students then may be encouraged to explore its implications for different cases in which a similar judgement might have different consequences. Students may be encouraged also to defend their judgement against the criticisms of their fellow-students and teachers, explaining their reasons in terms which would be comprehensible not only to their colleagues, but also to the average educated layman.

Summary

2.20 The scope of medical ethics teaching thus includes at least three elements: first, encouraging students to think for themselves about the range and variety of medico-moral questions; second, helping students become aware that these issues are not simply matters of personal opinion; and third, encouraging students to make, defend, criticise and reflect on the kind of moral judgements which medical practice will require of them. While it may be beyond the scope of medical ethics to include teaching on the skills and techniques of medical communication, the importance of developing these skills and techniques may be highlighted if students are asked, in addition, to explain the reasons for their moral judgements in simple, non-medical English.

REFERENCES

1. Edelstein, Ludwig (1967) 'The Hippocratic Oath: Text, Translation and Interpretation'; in Edelstein, L *Ancient Medicine* Baltimore, Johns Hopkins Press, pp 3–63
2. Newman, Lucille F (1978) 'History of Medical Ethics: Primitive Societies'; in Reich, Warren T (ed) *Encyclopaedia of Bioethics* New York, The Free Press, pp 877–879
3. Leake, Chauncey D (1975) *Percival's Medical Ethics* New York, Robert E Krieger Publishing Company.
4. Wolstenholme, Gordon (1978) 'History of Medical Ethics: Britain in the Twentieth Century'; in Reich *op. cit,* pp 987–991

CHAPTER THREE

Existing arrangements for medical ethics teaching

Introduction

3.1 This chapter summarises the Working Party's findings on present provision for the teaching of medical ethics in medical schools in the United Kingdom. It begins with a brief account of the antecedents and method of the enquiry (paragraphs 3.2 to 3.4). Next, it records the answers of Deans and medical students to questions about medical school policy, and timetabled and other teaching (paragraphs 3.6 to 3.14). Further evidence from Deans and students follows, on the involvement of non-medical teachers, examination questions and essays, project and elective work, and related extra-curricular activities (paragraphs 3.15 to 3.23). The Deans' evidence on relevant interest and training among their staff is summarised (3.24) and the views of Deans on ethics teaching are recorded (3.25 to 3.28). This is followed by some information about ethics courses for medical teachers (3.29), and evidence from junior hospital doctors (3.30). The chapter concludes with an account of the views on ethics teaching expressed by medical students (3.31 to 3.39), and a short summary (3.40).

Earlier information

3.2 Some information on existing arrangements for medical ethics teaching was included in the survey of basic medical education conducted by the General Medical Council in 1975-1976. In this survey however, because questionnaire replies on the two had overlapped, the 'topic' of medical ethics was discussed together with the speciality of forensic medicine: 'courses in traditional forensic medicine', the GMC reported, appeared 'to be diminishing in the UK', but there was 'disagreement as to how to replace them'[1]. Since 1976, reports on medical ethics teaching in a handful of British medical schools have been published[2], and in 1984 the GMC Education Committee held a conference on the subject[3]. But reliable information about existing arrangements in the majority of British medical schools was not readily available.

Questionnaires and consultations

3.3 Against this background, the Working Party decided to seek further information by questionnaires and other means. At the end of 1984, it sent a questionnaire on the teaching of medical ethics to the Deans of 30 British medical schools, of whom 26 replied.

Medical teachers nominated by the Deans subsequently met the Working Party to discuss some of their replies in greater detail. During 1985, a similar questionnaire was sent to medical student representatives (the Presidents of medical student unions in each of the British medical schools and student officers of Medical Groups) and 30 replies were received. Further information was gathered at three consultations with students and two with pre-registration house officers.

The questions

3.4 Deans and medical students were each asked seven questions. These concerned: 1) the school's policy on ethics teaching; 2) timetabled periods; 3) encouragement of informal discussion; 4) involvement of non-medical teachers; 5) assessment and encouragement of students' familiarity with ethical issues; 6) extra-curricular activities; and 7) the respondent's views on medical ethics teaching.

Replies of Deans and students: medical school policy

3.5 Asked if their school had any 'explicit policy ... to encourage the teaching or discussion of ethical issues within the medical course', most Deans responded by mentioning formal or informal provision made by curriculum committees or departments: but even the 6 Deans replying in the negative later indicated that some ethics teaching took place within their schools. In 3 London schools and 3 elsewhere, medical ethics teaching had been the subject of a recent internal enquiry, the conclusions of which had been or were about to be implemented. The replies of 3 English Provincial Deans included a statement of their school's general philosophy of medical education, emphasising scientific, humanitarian and professional standards. One Scottish Dean stated a specific policy of improving 'students' awareness of their own moral and ethical values and the fact that there is seldom a standard solution to major ethical questions in the care of individual patients'. Most Deans stressed the importance of integrating ethics with other clinical teaching, and in some cases with integrated pre-clinical teaching. One London school, however, regarded medical ethics as a 'required subject to be taught' at both stages of the curriculum, while another was considering, as a long-term objective, 'whether Moral Philosophy should be taught'. Student replies to a similar question, about their awareness of any medical school policy or encouragement of medical ethics teaching or discussion, were divided: 5 London students and 4 elsewhere replied in the negative, some emphatically; the remainder either inferred some such policy from timetabled ethics lectures and seminars, or simply stated that some clinicians dealt with the subject.

Deans' replies: timetabled periods

3.6 Asked about timetabled periods of formal medical ethics teaching, all of the Deans had something to report. In two cases this amounted to no more than 2 or 3 traditional final year lectures on professional ethics. But most schools reported rather more than this. All taught some traditional or professional ethics, either in introductory lectures at the beginning of clinical studies, or near their end in a medico-legal context. In addition to this, the majority reported some ethics teaching of a more problem-oriented kind. This might be organised on a departmental or a multidisciplinary basis, for whole years or for small groups, at fixed points in the curriculum or as sessions open to all students, as a separate subject or integrated with other teaching. Which of these options were chosen varied from school to school, depending either on the school's educational philosophy or on opportunity.

Deans' replies: professional ethics

3.7 Professional ethics was taught in introductory clinical lectures by 3 London schools (in 2 for 1 hour and in the other for 4). Three English Provincial schools each had 1 or 2 similar introductory lectures, while in a fourth, the subject was included in lectures (2½ hours) in Community Medicine. Three further London schools included topics such as consent and confidentiality in Forensic Medicine teaching (varying from 2 hours in one to 9 in another) near the end of clinical studies. Similar courses at this stage in the curriculum were reported by 7 schools (including the 3 with introductory lectures) in the English Provinces and Northern Ireland (in one case of unspecified length, in 3 of one lecture, and in the remainder of 5, 6 and 8 hours respectively). Forensic Medicine or medico-legal courses (of about 2 to 6 hours, but in one school of 20) were taught also in the 4th or 5th years of the four Scottish schools.

Deans' replies: Integrated teaching

3.8 In some schools, professional or problem-oriented ethics teaching accompanied an earlier introduction to clinical or community experience. Three English Provincial schools with more integrated curricula reported introductory lectures or discussions in the 1st and 2nd years: in one, there was a lecture on problems of clinical decision-making and then 4 lectures on drug and alcohol abuse, venereal disease and contraception; the second had a lecture on professional ethics (1 hour) and an illustrated discussion of neo-natal problems; the third included various seminars on ethical topics (6 hours). These schools emphasised that ethics teaching was not confined to these contexts: the ethics of medical research, for example, might be discussed in basic medical science teaching, or attitudes, communication and resource allocation in a community health course.

Deans' replies: small-group teaching

3.9 Two of these 3 schools emphasised also that small-group tutorials provided regular opportunities to discuss any ethical issue arising in the course. Small-group teaching, based on a supervisor system and clinical teams was reported by another Provincial school, while in the clinical curriculum of one London and a further Provincial school such teaching was undertaken by a particular surgical firm. In the London school, all students passed through the firm which spent 2, 3 and frequently more hours on ethical issues; in the Provincial school only half of the year were attached to the firm, but these had weekly tutorials on or involving ethical topics. Much informal clinical ethics teaching (see 3.13 below) was done in small groups also.

Deans' replies: departmental teaching

3.10 Timetabled departmental ethics teaching was reported by 6 London, 10 Provincial and 3 Scottish schools, but the number of hours assigned for this were specified only by the following. One London school had 12½ hours (4½ in pre-clinical Sociology and 8 in the 1st clinical year's General Practice); two others each had 3 hours (in General Practice and Obstetrics respectively) and a further school reported a lecture in Paediatrics. One Provincial school reported 10 hours in 4th year Obstetrics and another 2 final year lecture/discussions in terminal care. One Scottish school reported tutorial/case-conferences of 1 hour each in 4th year Obstetrics and Child Health, and of 5 hours in 5th year Medicine. A second had 10 hours (although only 2½ hours for each student) of multidisciplinary ethics sessions in year 3/4 Obstetrics and a tutorial (for half of the student year) in year 4/5 Obstetrics; this school also had 2 mornings in Geriatric Medicine, one on terminal care and the other of student presentations, mostly on ethical issues. From this school, Obstetrics, Geriatric Medicine and Community Medicine (see 3.11 below) were the only departments stating that they made timetabled provision for ethics, although most of the 21 departments which completed the questionnaire said that ethical issues were discussed in their teaching.

Deans' replies: multidisciplinary teaching

3.11 A number of schools recently had introduced multidisciplinary ethics teaching. The 1st year of the two Scottish schools just mentioned, for example, included 6 and 2 hours respectively: in the former this was followed by 3 hours of ethics seminars in 2nd year Behavioural Sciences, while in the latter, elective 1st year projects included 3 or 4 oriented to ethics. In a third Scottish school, the 2nd year included a lecture, seminar and examination question on the nature of moral argument, while 16 hours of lectures and seminars on ethics had just been introduced into 3rd year Medicine. A similar course, of 14 hours in the 4th year, had recently been included in a fourth Scottish school. Local Philosophy Departments made a significant contribution to teaching in these last two schools, while philosophers and theologians were involved in the other Scottish schools also. Innovatory multidisciplinary sessions were reported by 4 London schools and 3 elsewhere in England: most involved case presentations and discussion, two of the London schools also having an introduction or summing-up by a philosopher. The London sessions, held over several weeks near the beginning of the clinical course, in two schools each involved 8 hours teaching time, in a third 12 and in a fourth, 15. (The 15 hours however were at lunchtimes and one of the 8-hour series from 3.30 pm on Fridays.) Of the Provincial schools, one had 3 hours in its 4th year, a second 10 to 12 hours (involving Psychiatry, Medicine and General Practice) in its 3rd and final years, and a third reported a 4th year 10 hour course on Ethics and Legal Medicine involving multidisciplinary discussions. (The last course however, it was later reported, took place from 3pm to 5pm on Fridays and was voluntary.) Three further Provincial schools said that they had new courses planned: one was in medico-legal studies (including ethics), the second would have 2 or 3 days of workshops for 4th year students with Philosophy Department input, while the third would comprise daily sessions to discuss ethical issues arising during a reorganised 4-week introduction to clinical studies. Much of the multidisciplinary teaching mentioned in this paragraph appeared not to be examined; and the tutor responsible for one of the more ambitious English courses stated that many students 'did not perceive the course to be part of their *formal* curriculum'.

Deans' replies: open lectures and elective courses

3.12 Various open lectures and elective courses were reported. In London, one school held an annual guest lecture on ethics, another had 4 such open lectures and a third organised termly workshops open to students, hospital staff and the local community. One other English school held a twice-yearly series of 8 lunchtime lectures on medico-moral topics. This school also, uniquely, offered a course on Law and Ethics as a pre-clinical option. In one Scottish school, a series of 8 lectures on Logic in Medicine had been arranged, but was held at 5.15 pm and was badly attended by students. In all schools, these activities were in addition to those organised by local Medical Groups and student societies.

Deans' replies: informal discussion

3.13 Asked about the encouragement of informal discussion of ethical issues in departments or classes, the Deans were unable to provide any more particular evidence than has been noted in the preceding paragraphs. All of the schools stated or implied, as one London school put it, that 'few clinical teachers will fail to consider ethical issues from time to time'; and many suggested that the school or its departments encouraged this. One London school however, remarked that 'specific encouragement is not seen to be necessary, and might be seen as something of an insult by teachers who regard such aspects as integral in their approach to medicine and teaching'. But difficulties with this view were pointed out, in discussion with the Working Party, by medical teachers from two Provincial schools. One, chairman of his school's board of undergraduate studies, remarked: 'I **think** that these ethical issues are debated by clinicians with their firms, but the whole point is that I don't **know**'. The other had asked students about the ethics teaching reported by his colleagues. He had found that while 'some teachers claimed to be achieving something which students were quite blank about', there also 'were some teachers who claimed not to be teaching any ethics, from whom, students said, they had learned a great deal about various ethical principles and how they applied to certain sorts of case'.

Student impressions: timetabled periods and informal discussion

3.14 Asked about timetabled periods of formal medical ethics teaching 8 student respondents stated that they knew of none, and 4 of these students also stated that there was no encouragement of informal discussion. Of the remaining 19 students who knew of timetabled teaching, 5 stated that informal discussion of ethical issues was not encouraged. Replies from students who knew of timetabled teaching gave the impression of similar kinds of teaching as those reported by the Deans, although students tended to be more minimalist (e.g. 'it was just a few points – included legislation, the Anatomy Act and the legal position of the doctor') and to point out difficulties (e.g. 'In the first year the odd ethical topic was scheduled on Wednesday morning – it didn't fit in with anatomy, biochemistry, physiology etc – similarly with the second year'). Students who thought that informal discussion was encouraged tended to see this being done either in particular departments (reflecting the Deans' replies to 3.10 above) or by 'interested consultants'. Positive replies related to the latter varied from 'we glean some ethical points from most ward rounds, with an occasional dissertation from the consultant on a particular ethical aspect of difficult medical practice', to 'during ward rounds senior staff may discuss moral/ethical problems if pushed by a highly motivated student – often such questions are frowned upon not only by the members of staff but also by fellow students'. The latter view was more strongly reflected in the student consultations, which elicited experience from schools across the country of the difficulties faced by students on wards with clinicians (frequently registrars) who avoided or responded badly to ethical questions. Elsewhere, on the other hand, 'interested' clinicians clearly were highly effective. The consultations also confirmed the impression that students generally were aware of the kinds of teaching reported by the Deans. But doubts were expressed about how much of this teaching concerned ethics rather than, for example, sociology, law, terminal care and communication.

Deans' replies: involvement of non-medical teachers

3.15 Asked if non-medical persons were involved in ethics teaching, only two schools replied in the negative. At least 6, however, either did not answer this question or replied in terms of involvement in extracurricular activities, including those of the local Medical Group. The contexts in which non-medical persons were involved varied from that of health visitors in a Genito-Urinary Department's teaching on contact tracing and counselling, to that of a Philosophy Department in a course specifically on ethics. The non-medical persons mentioned were from a variety of disciplines. Nine schools mentioned their own non-medical scientific or behavourial science staff, and 2 spoke of other hospital staff. Nurses or health visitors were mentioned by 6 schools, social workers by 7, chaplains or clergy by 6, and patients or representives of patients' organisations by 5. Theologians were said to be involved in teaching in 3 schools, philosophers in 8 and lawyers in 5 (in 4 of these the same lawyer was mentioned).

Student impressions: involvement of non-medical teachers

3.16 Among the student respondents, 11 replied that no non-medical persons were involved in ethics teaching. Two mentioned non-medical involvement in Medical Groups, one referred to 'other students in the debating society', and another remarked that four lectures by a member of the Education Department had been 'non-examined' and had 'poor attendance'. Positive replies included an unspecified 'some' and mention, by 6 respondents, of non-medical scientific and behavourial science staff. Renal Medicine, Oncology and Mental Handicap respectively, were specified in 3 responses as the context of teaching involving nurses, social workers, counsellors and relatives; although the first of these respondents added that there was 'very limited reference to ethics *per se*'. In another school's Sociology course 'a more legal view of medical ethics' was given by a law professor, and 'pharmaceutical-related persons gave talks' on medical ethics in a biometrics course. Two students reported involvement of a hospital chaplain, in one case discussing neonatal death; while 2 other respondents each knew of tutorials run by philosophers. Further lawyers had been among one student's teachers in an elective pre-clinical course.

Deans' replies: examinations and essays

3.17 Asked if 'familiarity of students with ethical issues' was 'ascertained by including reference to these in written or oral examinations', 11 schools replied in positive terms. Most of these expected some awareness of ethical issues to be demonstrated by students. But 6 schools included either examination questions or essay titles specifically on ethical topics: integrated teaching, departmental teaching, continuous assessment and final examinations were, variously, mentioned as the locus; while in 2 Scottish schools an essay was required as part of an ethics course. Replies from 5 schools suggested that awareness of ethical issues was, or might be, taken into account when assessing the clinical competence of students.

Student impressions: examinations and essays

3.18 Among the student respondents, 16 replied to this question in negative terms, in some cases adding 'as far as I know'. Of the

11 positive replies, 2 thought that familiarity with ethical issues was assessed through informal testing of clinical competence, while a further 6 reported this being done through continuous assessment or oral examinations. Some of these and other respondents reported written examination questions or essays: in two cases these were in Forensic Medicine; a third was an ethics essay in a medico-legal elective course. One Sociology course had an essay question on ethics, as had one Community Medicine course. One respondent stated that 'in Chemical Pathology we were told that some questions may be answered from an ethical as opposed to a scientific angle'. Another reported that examinations in Medicine and Geriatrics included questions about, respectively, 'factors to consider in telling a person he was going to die', and 'the quality not quantity of life argument'. A student respondent from a school with 14 hours of medical ethics teaching involving the Philosophy Department, reported that a compulsory question on medical ethics was included in an examination contributing to the final in Medicine and Surgery; there was also a course essay.

Essay titles and examination questions

3.19 The essay mentioned at the end of the last paragraph might be written on one of the following questions, the student reported:
a) What problems arise in deciding what constitutes 'dying well'?
b) Has a doctor a right to withhold the truth from his patient?
c) 'The primary duty of the physician is to act in the best interests of the patient as the patient himself views those best interests'. Do you agree?
d) What moral limits should there be to medical research?
e) What principles should govern the allocation of limited resources in medicine?
In another school with Philosophy Department involvement in teaching, a pre-clinical examination question was:

Either   Briefly outline some moral principles which might be relevant to moral dilemmas in medicine. Describe a medical situation in which two of them might seem to conflict. How, if at all, can such disputes be resolved?

Or   A spokesman for the Ethical Committee of the B.M.A. is reported as having said of virginity tests carried out on Asian women at Heathrow Airport that while they may have been morally wrong there was nothing unethical about them. (*World Medicine*, March 10 1979, p99) In what sense(s), if any, is it helpful to distinguish 'morals' and 'ethics'?

The Professor of Philosophy involved over three years in this course, reported to the Working Party that about 90% of the class attempted the ethics question. He wrote:

> The standard was excellent. They had *learned* the material in the lecture, *used* it in seminar discussions and *adapted* it to their experience. The exam answers were quite comparable to a first year moral philosophy exam.

Deans' replies: projects and electives

3.20 Asked if familiarity with ethical issues was encouraged by project work, elective work, elective study or any other method, 11 schools replied in the affirmative. Most of these mentioned elective study or project work, mainly in Behavourial Sciences, Community Medicine, General Practice, Obstetrics, Paediatrics and Psychiatry. One school stated that the occasional student might choose to do a 3-month elective in medical ethics and two spoke of possibilities during the intercalated year. Very few schools specified 'other' methods: one provided all clinical students with a copy of the B.M.A.'s *Handbook of Medical Ethics*, while another mentioned students winning Medical Defence Union prizes or being asked to provide cases for medico-moral case conferences. One school's reply included the comment, from an orthopaedic surgeon, that familiarity with ethical issues was encouraged 'principally by the method of "osmosis" during clinical teaching of medical students'.

Student impressions: projects and electives

3.21 Of the student replies to this question, 17 were in negative terms, again with the proviso that there might be opportunities which the respondent had not yet encountered. Of the 11 positive replies, 4 stated that project or elective work on ethical issues was possible but not specifically encouraged, while another stated that it was encouraged. One respondent wrote that 'a study of medical ethics relating to children' was 'acceptable' for a compulsory Paediatric project, 2 mentioned General Practice and 1, Community Medicine projects on ethical issues; and a further respondent reported that 'some projects on firms are meant to cover ethical topics'. One student commented:

> Most electives in third world countries will bring you into contact with different ideas of what is right or wrong. I think this is more valuable than spending two months specifically studying ethics from a cosy room in England.

Deans' replies: extra-curricular activities

3.22 Asked 'what encouragement is given to students to participate in extra-curricular activities relevant to ethics(e.g. The London or other Medical Groups)', 21 of the 26 Deans who responded, replied that students were encouraged to participate in their local Medical Group, and that many members of staff also participated. The Deans of 2 other schools with a local Medical Group did not answer this question specifically. There was no Medical Group in the remaining 3 schools: one was pre-clinical only, the second stated that 'the Christian Fellowship, Inter-faculty Christian Union and the "Questioning Medicine Group"' had 'fully served the needs of some students for discussion'; and the third school indicated an intention to arrange some voluntary lectures in the next academic year. In this context, 4 schools again mentioned their own open lectures (noted under 3.12 above). One school stated that its Medical Group 'effectively produces a good "alternative curriculum"'.

Student impressions: extra-curricular activities

3.23 Students were asked the same question, but without specific reference to Medical Groups. Five replied that no encouragement was given, one said there was 'moderate' and another 'every' encouragement. Six stated that encouragement was given by Medical Group representatives, and 8 that staff encouraged attendance at Medical Group lectures and symposia. Four mentioned encouragement by or of Christian societies, and 4 mentioned other student societies. One remarked that 'free pamphlets by the Medical Protection Society' were 'quite useful'.

Deans' replies: interested and trained staff

3.24 The Deans were asked to give details of members of their staff: a) who were particularly interested in ethics teaching and had developed teaching material on the topic; and b) who had any training in the teaching of medical ethics. The first part of the question was answered positively by 20 Deans, each of whom named between 1 and 8 members of their staff, and in 2 cases their University's Professor of Philosophy. Of the 20 Deans, 11 knew of no staff with training in ethics teaching. In 5 of the 9 schools with trained staff, the training had been received at the Imperial College/Institute of Medical Ethics Intensive Courses in Medical Ethics for Medical and Nursing Teachers (see 3.29 below). The relevant training for staff mentioned by the 4 remaining schools was not specified: they included two general practitioners, a geriatrician and a surgeon, each of whom had either served on working parties concerned with medical ethics, or written on the subject. The only individual with such training mentioned by one school was a lecturer in ethics from its associated school of nursing.

Deans' views: curricular opportunities

3.25 Asked for their views on the teaching of ethics to medical students, most Deans considered it 'important' or 'essential' that provision for this should be made within the curriculum; and some thought that greater provision should be made. Several others, however, echoed the Dean who added: 'Whether enough time can be set aside for this aspect of education in an already crowded curriculum is another matter'. One reply suggested that the ideal might be if 'those occasions which arise during the course of a medical student's training here in which ethical issues are involved' could be 'formalised without any major reconstruction of the existing medical curriculum'. The notion of formalising opportunities 'for students to learn and gradually develop their own attitude to ethical issues' was mentioned by several others. Often, this was contrasted with the idea of introducing ethics as a 'separate subject'. This last, particularly in the form of 'a structured lecture-type course', found little favour.

Deans' views: clinical and pre-clinical teaching

3.26 Clinical teaching, particularly in small groups, the Deans were agreed, was the best context in which students might learn about ethics. But as one reply observed, it was 'difficult to assess accurately the extent to which ethical issues are covered in the informal clinical and other teaching which takes place in the Faculty'. Moreover, while 'pre-clinical departments tend to feel that ethical issues are most appropriately dealt with in the context of clinical care and management', many clinicians were 'increasingly recognising that students need to be provided with a framework for ethical decision-making'. Thus while, as one respondent put it, 'the majority of teaching should be patient-related', there was also

> a need to provide early in the curriculum some formal instruction to introduce our students ... to the vocabulary of ethics, as well as identifying areas of ethical interest which they should know about when they receive their clinical instruction throughout the rest of the course.

Similar observations were made by others who stated, for example, that it was 'essential that students be introduced through discussion to ethical matters at a very early stage of the medical course'; and that it was necessary both to 'impart awareness of these issues' and to 'endow students with the intellectual resources to enable them to respond consistently and logically'.

Deans' views: student needs and assessment

3.27 Medical ethics teaching, different respondents suggested, should be concerned not only with 'principles of critical analysis', but also with students' need for the 'time and opportunity to open up their own fears and uncertainties in the face of topics like disability, death and dying'. At present it might be 'difficult to estimate' the effects of such teaching. But it was important that there should be some form of assessment, in order that ethics should not 'be seen as yet another optional extra'.

Deans' views: teachers, and teaching teachers

3.28 On the question of who should teach medical ethics, one Dean spoke favourably of the involvement of other professionals, including those from Nursing and Law. Another believed that teaching about the 'principles of ethical analysis ... would have more impact if taught by a clinician rather than by, say, a lawyer or philosopher'. But a third believed that it was helpful to include, in a case conference setting, 'a didactic contribution from a qualified teacher of ethics'. The same reply suggested that

> such an expert in medical ethics might be involved in the teaching and discussion of ethical issues with the senior members of staff interested in developing their knowledge and their expertise in this area.

This view was reflected in a fourth response, which stated:

> Perhaps the teachers need a refresher course so that they may apply (their knowledge) in a better informed way in clinical teaching.

Courses for teachers

3.29 Present provision of courses in ethics for medical teachers was subsequently investigated by the Working Party. Four courses were identified.
1) The Society of Apothecaries of London has a two-year course (held on Saturdays of alternate weekends) leading to its postgraduate Diploma in the Philosophy of Medicine, and attracting from 8 to 25 students.
2) Imperial College, London, in association with the Institute of Medical Ethics, has since 1983 held an annual Intensive Course in

Medical Ethics for Medical and Nursing Teachers: the course comprises multidisciplinary lectures and seminars on philosophical aspects of medico-moral problems, designed to help teaching in this area. Each course has places for about 30 participants.

3) King's College, London, since 1984, has held a half-day a week one-year course leading to a postgraduate Diploma in Medical Ethics and Law. It plans to convert this to an M A as from October 1986.

4) In 1985, University College, Cardiff instituted a two-year part-time scheme of study for the degree of M.A. in the Philosophy of Health Care: the degree is examined both by written papers and by dissertation; lectures are organised in six three-day residential sessions, supplemented by regular regional tutorials.

All four courses were found to be well-subscribed and sometimes over-subscribed, with the Cardiff course catering for the largest numbers. It had over 200 firm applications for its first year, on which 106 students were given places: these included approximately 32 hospital consultants, 18 general practitioners, 25 senior nurses, 8 hospital administrators and various other health care professionals, from different parts of the United Kingdom.

Deans' views: junior hospital doctors

3.30 A related topic was mentioned, in reply to the Working Party's questionnaire, by one Scottish Dean, who wrote:

Teaching of this topic (ethics) to graduates, particularly junior hospital doctors and young general practitioners, is also very important and requires assessment.

While the Working Party was primarily concerned with undergraduate teaching, it investigated this question subsequently by means of consultations with pre-registration house officers in hospitals associated with two medical schools. The house officers were asked: a) what kinds of ethical problem arose in their present work; b) whether their undergraduate training prepared them for this; and c) if they took advice about these problems and from whom. In reply to the first question, the house officers mentioned such issues as 'telling an untruth' to a terminally ill patient 'in his best interests', 'protecting a colleague to relatives while believing that colleague was negligent', 'asking for a postmortem and making relatives feel guilty for refusing': in general, the house officers' discussion of ethical questions constantly returned to the question of communication skills. Answers to the question about undergraduate preparation for these problems indicated that what the housemen remembered as most helpful in this context was teaching on communication skills and technique. As one group of house officers put it: 'ethics equals accommodating the patients' personal interests'. The same group, in reply to the question about advice, indicated that if the advice was about a question of policy (for example about the management of dying patients) on a new ward, they would ask the ward sister. 'If pushed', they would ask the consultant. But this, they said, 'takes courage', and although the consultant 'would be helpful if asked', there was 'certainly no expectation that senior medical staff have any responsibility to discuss such issues. '"Making difficult decisions" or "telling patients and relatives"', they believed, was 'part of becoming an experienced doctor and not something which can be taught'. Another group of house officers, who did not tackle the question about advice in any detail, indicated its relevance by deciding as a result of the consultation (held in the Dean's office) to repeat the exercise 'at three-monthly intervals to use as a forum for exchange of ideas and for discussing particular ethical problems which are confronting the housemen at the moment'.

Students' views: missed opportunities

3.31 Expressing their views on ethics teaching, student respondents to the Working Party's questionnaire agreed that an awareness of moral as well as medico-legal issues was necessary 'to enable (students) to deal with situations that will confront them in their career'. They agreed also that it was important for students to learn 'to think for themselves' about medical ethics, rather than to 'simply accept the practices employed by the hospitals in which they study'. Some respondents doubted whether students would do this unless 'challenged/inspired to do so'. Because their minds were 'normally pumped full of academic facts', many medical students were 'very narrowminded' and 'never question anything which will not have an immediate personal effect on themselves'. Matters were not necessarily helped, moreover, by their teachers. The 'passive learning process' in which 'clinicians teach by setting an example', had 'an element of hit and miss, as not all clinicians, by any means, set a good example'. The wards, where 'small groups of students... often well-known to each other' came 'face to face with specific problems' provided 'an ideal environment... for discussion of ethical issues'. But

> too often, opportunities for discussion are missed, due to lack of motivation on the part of staff and students.

Student views: unsympathetic to 'ethics teaching'

3.32 These views, however, were not shared by other student respondents. 'Informal ethical discussion on ward rounds', one wrote, 'usually arises without the clinicians having to be told to "teach the students ethics"'. Indeed, another remarked,

> I would find it almost insulting if I was taught ethics at college, as if I were unable or insufficently interested to formulate my own opinions.

After all, observed a third, 'medical students do occasionally think and will have their own moral principles'; and a fourth respondent summed up his view by writing

> A lot of 'ethics' is really common sense and by the time a student graduates I think that he knows all that he needs about ethics.

This view of ethics was developed by several respondents who wrote that ethics could not be taught, not least because 'everyone has their own different ethics'. These students thought that 'ethics teaching' meant teaching 'one view', by 'didactic' lectures, in a 'rigid "medical ethics teaching" timetable', or 'a specific "medical ethics course"'. Because of this, one argued that 'the teaching of medical ethics will fail unless it is voluntary'. But even this student recognised that 'there will always be those who avoid voluntary teaching'; and as another remarked, 'attending voluntary lectures for interest is a habit of the minority'.

Student views: more sympathetic

3.33 The majority of the student respondents, however, believed that 'there should be some formal teaching in medical ethics', provided that the 'danger of over-formalising and reducing discussion as with the rest of medical education' was avoided. Some suggested that 'the principles involved should be introduced to students' with 'time for informal discussion'; others that 'the existing viewpoints and alternatives should be aired, allowing the student to reach his own conclusion'. As one student put it

> Compassion and humility can't be taught, but if students are aware of options and their consequences, then a more informed course can be taken.

Student views: pre-clinical and clinical teaching

3.34 Several respondents were in favour of some formal pre-clinical sessions, 'introductory lectures', or 'a short series of general lectures followed up in the relevant departments'. Time for this might be provided, one suggested, by dropping 'some of the Sociology and some time-wasting practicals in Biochemistry and Physiology'. Students with experience of clinical tutorials with input from philosophers wrote that these had been particularly helpful; and small-group teaching generally was preferred to lectures; although debates 'in response to student demand' had 'often been valuable'. In clinical teaching, it was suggested, 'consultants should actively encourage discussion, especially after wardrounds and clinics in which the issues have arisen'. One respondent (unlike the student quoted in 3.32 above) even suggested that 'there could be an official directive from the college to the clinical teachers to have some discussion on ethics in the clinical teaching'.

Student views: teachers and teaching teachers

3.35 Students' views on who ought to teach ethics varied. One respondent remarked:

> many consultants are autocratic enough in matters of objective clinical practice without encouraging them to hold forth on matters of more subjective content.

Another, more enigmatically commented, 'I think that one lecture from a man like Professor X is probably adequate'. The ideal, the first student suggested, was

> to have someone presiding with both a thorough knowledge of the practicalities of the particular situation and also a sound philosophical/logical approach to the question of ethics. Many doctors seem to be reasonably (or very) competent in the former but to have no idea about the workings of moral philosophy or a study of ethics, and are therefore unable to sort out and present these ideas clearly enough.

A further respondent agreed.

> Our clinical teachers are not taught ethics. Teach *them* first, or rather expose them to moral issues in medicine of which they have only a brief and superficial awareness. If a greater ethical awareness in them alters their practice of medicine, then they will naturally expose their students to it.

Student views: examination questions

3.36 Five student respondents specifically mentioned examinations in reply to the question about their views on teaching. Two advocated an ethics question in General Medicine or finals papers. A third, (believing it 'difficult to draw up a formal examination, certainly of a Multiple Choice variety, in a subject where there is often no "right" or "wrong" answer') advocated an essay or project. Assessment was necessary, a further student commented, because 'often one hears students say, "This is not examinable, therefore there's no need to attend"'. Another agreed:

The course trains students to think 'fact' and everything learnt is related to examination. Either 'ethics' should be examinable (turning it into valuable information in the minds of students), or it must be made very relevant and related to medical events students have experience of.

Student consultations

3.37 Many of the impressions gained from the student questionnaire were endorsed by students attending the three consultations, two of which were organised by the Working Party, and the third by the student Association of Provincial Medical Schools. Student views on medical ethics teaching again reflected a variety of different experiences of medical education, and also the fear that 'medical ethics teaching' implied 'didactic' teaching of 'one view'. Examples of the latter, it was agreed, were sometimes found among teachers with a particular religious, philosophical or political commitment. But such an approach seemed uncharacteristic of most advocates and practitioners of medical ethics teaching; and after discussion, the students at one of the Working Party's consultations formulated the aims of medical ethics teaching as follows:

a)   to enable and encourage students
    i)   to think clearly and rationally
    ii) to examine the basis of their own beliefs and responses
    iii) to adopt a critical outlook
b)   to increase awareness of medical ethics issues.

Critical experiences

3.38 Students at the consultations recognised that the specific nature and timing of medical ethics teaching would depend on each school's particular curriculum. But although this varied, there were certain critical times in every student's career when opportunity should be provided to reflect on what was being experienced and to discuss its moral implications. Examples of these were experience of dissection, early ward experience, the first encounter with a psychiatric patient, the first death of a patient with whom the student had been particularly involved, and experience of a termination of pregnancy.

Student recommendations

3.39 Students at each of the consultations recorded various recommendations on ethics teaching. While students attending the

Working Party's consultations were more inclined to argue that an examination question or essay on an ethical topic should be compulsory, their general views were reflected in the recommendations of the student Association of Provincial Medical Schools. The Association believed that present provision for medical ethics teaching was 'insufficient'. Medical ethics teaching, it argued, should encourage 'the development of methods of thought directed towards the evaluation of moral issues'. This teaching, at both undergraduate and post-graduate levels, should involve both clinicians and philosophers as teachers, who should 'act by leading discussions and small group seminars and by criticising any essays which students may agree to write'. The Association considered it 'acceptable for assessments to be made by criticism of essays'. Time should be found for students to discuss problems which they had 'encountered in the course of their clinical work'. Before engaging in medical ethics teaching, medical teachers should 'take courses in medical ethics'.

Summary

3.40 Evidence to the Working Party suggests that most British medical schools now include some problem-oriented as well as traditional medical ethics teaching in their undergraduate curricula. The total number of timetabled periods of ethics teaching is not large however. The amount of informal discussion of ethical topics encouraged by clinical teachers is difficult to estimate, but appears to range from the regular to the non-existent. Ethics teaching is encouraged particularly by such Departments as Obstetrics, Paediatrics, General Practice and Community Medicine, and in a few schools, short ethics courses have been introduced: in both of these contexts, non-medical teachers are normally involved. Very few medical teachers appear to have any specific training in medical ethics teaching. While most schools see a role for extra-curricular activities in student learning about medical ethics, some now also include reference to ethical issues in examinations. Most Deans consider ethics teaching 'important', but are doubtful about introducing it as a 'separate subject': most lay emphasis on informal clinical teaching, sensitive to students' needs, but also including some academic assessment. Student views on these matters are not markedly different, although some students are critical of their experience of informal clinical teaching. Didactic or ideological teaching is generally suspect. Some training in ethics teaching for medical teachers is generally favoured.

REFERENCES

1. General Medical Council (1977) *Basic Medical Education in the British Isles*, London, Nuffield Provincial Hospitals Trust, p.448.
2. Jones J S P Metcalfe D H H (1976) 'The teaching of medical ethics in the Nottingham Medical School' *Journal of Medical Ethics* 2.2. 83-86.
   Dennis K J and Hall M R P (1977) 'The teaching of medical ethics at Southampton University Medical School' *Journal of Medical Ethics* 3.4. 183-185.
   Boyd K, Currie C, Tierney A and Thompson I E (1978) 'The teaching of medical ethics: University of Edinburgh' *Journal of Medical Ethics* 4.3. 141-145.
3. *Journal of Medical Ethics* (1985) 11.1.

CHAPTER FOUR

Recommendations

Medical ethics teaching

4.1 Medical ethics is central to the practice of medicine and its implications should be made explicit throughout medical education. The teaching of medical ethics should not be seen primarily in terms of a new subject to be added to the curriculum, and for this reason the Working Party has decided against recommending a specific syllabus for medical ethics. At present, medical ethics teaching will best be encouraged by encouraging local initiatives, making use of opportunities created within the resources available to each medical school. With these considerations in mind, the Working Party's first and most general recommendation is that:

1. **Medical ethics teaching should recur at regular intervals throughout medical training, and time should be set aside within existing teaching for ethical reflection relevant to each stage of the student's experience.**

Clinical teaching

4.2 Clinical teaching is central to medical education and it is of first importance that ethical issues should be raised as a regular part of routine clinical teaching. While clinical teaching strategies will vary from school to school, some options are more conducive than others to what the Working Party envisages as the aims of medical ethics education (see 2.20 above). The Working Party recommends that:

2. **Clinical teaching of ethics should normally begin from clinical examples. Such teaching should be exploratory and analytical rather than hortatory. Adequate provision should be made for small-group discussion. Discussion should be supported by critical reading of relevant papers on medical ethics.**

This recommendation is designed to facilitate the general method of teaching which the Working Party envisages (see 2.19 above). It is made also, in response to the need expressed by many medical students (see 3.38 above) for time and the opportunity to reflect on formative experiences in their training and to discuss the moral implications of these experiences.

Pre-clinical teaching

4.3 These experiences may be occasioned from the earliest stages of the pre-clinical curriculum. In traditional curricula they include, for example, the experience of dissection; while in integrated curricula, or those with early clinical or community experience, formative encounters with patients may take place. What has been said about clinical teaching thus may apply to pre-clinical also. One advantage of a case-based approach to pre-clinical ethics teaching (as described at one of the Working Party's student consultations) is that it 'puts clinical material into behavourial science'. On the other hand, the pre-clinical curriculum may afford opportunities for a general introduction to th nature of moral argument which (again to quote one of the student consultations) 'might help to keep alive original thought during the cramming of the first two years'. Given the variety of educational strategies adopted in the early years of different medical schools, the Working Party does not feel able to make specific recommendations about pre-clinical ethics teaching which would be generally applicable. In general terms however, it envisages that pre-clinical teaching might usefully include some didactic presentation of the 'body of knowledge' concerning the nature of moral argument (see 2.18 above) as well as of the requirements of professional medical ethics.

Medical teachers

4.4 The Working Party has concluded from its enquiries that clinical teaching, at its best, already raises ethical issues on a regular and routine basis. Neither the Working Party nor anyone else, however, knows how often the best is achieved. Certainly there seem to be times when it is not, and thus when medical students are inadequately prepared for the moral dilemmas of medical practice. One reason for inadequate clinical teaching of ethics appears to be that many medical teachers lack experience of the vocabulary of ethics. With such experience, clinical teachers would have greater confidence to discuss the different sides of relevant moral questions, in terms more helpful to themselves, their students and their patients. Without it, in present-day society, doctors will become increasingly vulnerable to the criticism that they are poor communicators or inappropriately paternalistic.

Training in ethics

4.5 The experience required, the Working Party believes, may be gained either by further training or by teaching itself. For some clinicians, it may involve attendance at courses of the kind mentioned in 3.29 above. The Working Party recommends that:

3. **Interested medical teachers should be encouraged and assisted to undertake further study of medical ethics in the context of courses already available.**

The creation of further courses may be desirable, but subject to provisos of the kind noted in 4.9 below.

Training traditional teachers

4.6 Training in ethics is particularly desirable for clinicians whose teaching is of a traditional, opportunistic kind. Where most teaching is done on the wards, the opportunities to discuss ethical issues have to be exploited as they arise. Clinical teachers with training in ethics are likely to be sensitive to the kinds of moral argument which particular clinical examples involve. Thus they will be in a good position to help their students understand the strengths and weaknesses of these arguments. Such teaching, moreover, can help students work through their own reactions at critical points in their personal and professional development.

Multidisciplinary teaching

4.7 In the foreseeable future, only a minority of clinical teachers are likely to be able to undertake training in ethics. For the majority, useful experience may be gained by involvement in regular multidisciplinary teaching. The Working Party recommends that:

4. **Multidisciplinary ethics teaching sessions should be timetabled at regular intervals within existing clinical teaching. These sessions should normally involve a teacher or teachers with training in the analytic disciplines (moral philosophy, moral theology or law) and, when appropriate, representatives of the professions associated with medicine (nursing, social work, chaplaincy and others), together with representatives of articulate and considered lay opinion.**

Departmental and integrated teaching

4.8 How this recommendation is implemented will depend on the educational strategy and resources of each medical school. In those with a discipline-based curriculum, clinical teaching in each of the major specialities might include at least one multidisciplinary session. This would review the ethical implications of what students have learnt and experienced in the

37

relevant department, possibly with students presenting cases. In addition to departmental teaching however, some opportunity should be provided for ethical reflection on themes common to all the specialities. These (as mentioned in 2.15 above) would include clinical competence, consent, confidentiality, communication and priorities. In schools with an integrated curriculum, these common themes might provide the focus for interdepartmental as well as multidisciplinary sessions; although in these schools, some place also would need to be found for consideration of moral issues of special concern to particular specialities.

Careful planning

4.9 When setting up multidisciplinary sessions or courses, it should be borne in mind that some teachers from non-medical disciplines may lack the experience of clinical realities required to teach ethics effectively to medical students. Not all philosophers, theologians, lawyers or other non-medical teachers, moreover, have ethics as their main teaching interest. Thus while it may be possible to recruit non-medical teachers locally to undertake ethics teaching, not all these necessarily will have appropriate experience or training. The Working Party recommends that:

5. **Courses introducing students to ethics should not be undertaken without careful planning, drawing on the experience of other schools and bodies (including the Institute of Medical Ethics) already involved in medical ethics teaching.**

Against ideologues

4.10 Careful planning is necessary not only for multidisciplinary teaching, but also for medical ethics teaching in general. That an individual medical teacher or ethics teacher is willing to undertake ethics teaching, again is not sufficient. The Working Party recommends that:

6. **Care should be taken to avoid leaving ethics teaching in the hands of a teacher whose tendency is to promote a single political, religious or philosophical viewpoint.**

While dangers of allowing this in the case of political or religious ideologues may be obvious, it may not be apparent immediately that even some lawyers or philosophers may not always be as even-handed as their profession suggests.

Timetabling

4.11 A further aspect of planning ethics teaching relates to the practicalities of timetabling. The Working Party recommends that:

7. **Those planning ethics teaching should bear in mind that the importance attached to a subject is clearly reflected in the hour or day set aside for it.**

Examinations, essays, projects

4.12 In not recommending a specific syllabus for medical ethics teaching, the Working Party is aware that the academic standing of medical ethics may seem to be left in question. It recommends, therefore that:

8. **Examination questions or essays (and where appropriate, project work) on ethical issues should be included in the assessment leading to a medical qualification. The purpose of such assessment should be to verify that students are able to think critically and logically about ethical issues in medicine in the light of counterarguments to their own position.**

Elective courses

4.13 The unamended methods, content and illustrative material of undergraduate teaching in departments of law, philosophy or theology may well not be appropriate for the medical curriculum. These may be appropriate however, for individual medical students wishing to study ethics more systematically on an elective basis. The Working Party recommends that:

9. **Interested medical students should be encouraged and assisted to undertake elective courses arranged by or in co-operation with departments of philosophy, theology and law.**

This could have the additional benefit, eventually, of increasing the proportion of clinical teachers with some training in ethics.

Extra-curricular learning

4.14 The recommendations above are about medical ethics teaching within the curriculum. But a significant contribution to student learning in this area is made also by extra-curricular study and discussion, in particular that sponsored by the student Medical Groups. While these activities normally attract only a small proportion of medical students, their influence extends more widely. Participation in Medical Group activities, for example, has introduced many students and teachers to the language of ethics, in ways which have proved useful within the curriculum. In a number of cases, moreover, staff associated with a Medical Group have stimulated and participated in curricular ethics teaching, the multidisciplinary Medical Group network proving particularly useful in this connection. Most important, perhaps, is that Medical Groups provide a student critique of medical practice. This last might well be lost if all medical ethics learning were to be subjected to the pressures of the curriculum. The Working Party recommends that:

10. **Medical ethics teaching within the curriculum should not be regarded as superseding the unique contribution of student Medical Groups to medical ethics teaching and learning.**

Continuing education

4.15 In making its recommendations about undergraduate medical education, the Working Party is aware of and wishes to endorse the statement recorded earlier (3.30 above) that 'teaching of (ethics) to graduates, particularly junior hospital doctors and young general practitioners, is also very important and requires assessment'. The Working Party recommends that:

11. **The Institute of Medical Ethics approach post-graduate medical bodies with a view to undertaking a study of ethics teaching in continuing education.**

Subject to review

4.16 The Working Party has consciously refrained from proposing a model curriculum which would have demanded the negotiation of time for a new subject. The recommendations above, moreover, are intended to be reviewed, say, in five years time. On the other hand, they are recommendations designed to be within the scope of every medical school in the United Kingdom. In addition however, the Working Party recommends that:

12. **The Institute of Medical Ethics should undertake a further reassessment of teaching options and of the Working Party's own recommendations in five year's time. In the meantime, the Institute should write annually to the Deans of medical schools, enquiring about new developments in medical ethics teaching; the information received should be published in the IME Bulletin.**

APPENDICES

APPENDIX ONE

More detailed information about Deans' replies to the working party's question: 'What timetabled periods of formal teaching are there — please state which departments, years of courses, hours allocated, methods used?'

Replies from schools in London

1.1   In London, the smallest number of medical ethics teaching hours was reported by a school which had two 1-hour lectures in the final clinical year. What appeared to be the largest number was reported by a school whose ethics teaching included: a) an introductory clinical course lecture; b) departmental ethics teaching in Oncology, Haematology and Clinical Pharmacology; c) visits to hospices with lectures on bereavement and counselling; d) 4 medical ethics lectures annually for all students; and e) a 10-week course of 1½-hour seminars for students beginning their clinical studies. These seminars, led by a philosopher and a GP with other clinicians participating, each comprised a 20-minute lecture on an ethical issue, followed by a 20- or 30-minute film illustrating the problem, and concluding with 30 to 40 minutes of discussion. Begun in 1985, the course had 75% student attendence. Most students however, reported that they did not undertake the suggested background reading: among the reasons for this, the course director believed, was that the students 'did not perceive the course to be part of their **formal** curriculum', perhaps because it was held from 12.30 pm until 2 pm.

1.2   Two other London schools reported a relatively large number of hours. In one, the relevant teaching (in addition to that by individual teachers in a variety of clinical departments) included: a) 2 lectures (4½ hours) by a GP and a lawyer in the pre-clinical Sociology course; b) 8 small-group seminars (8 hours) in first clinical year General Practice; and c) 8 topic teaching sessions (8 hours) at the end of the first clinical year. The last, including symposia, medico-moral case conferences and lectures, was attended also by nursing students. The other school, in October 1985, expanded teaching during the final pre-clinical and first clinical terms, to include 8 1½-hour sessions in medical ethics. These each began with a case presentation by a clinical team (including nurses, social workers and students): general discussion followed, and the session concluded with 'a more didactic presentation' by a moral philosopher. These sessions were in addition to existing ethics teaching of up to 3 hours in second clinical year General Practice and Psychiatry, and other more informal discussions of ethics in the teaching of different clinical departments.

1.3   The replies from two further London schools focussed on sessions in the first clinical year. One of the schools organised 4 lectures on decision-making, confidentiality, consent and the patient's viewpoint (given by someone who had recently been a patient) and terminal care. There was also a lecture in Paediatrics and an annual guest lecture. Otherwise students were expected 'to learn by example/experience'. The other school included four 45-minute sessions in its main clinical lecture course. These began with a videotaped discussion between a clinician, student and patient, followed by general discussion. In Forensic Medicine, there were 6 formal lectures followed by ½-hour discussions, covering codes, consent, confidentiality and medical responsibility, all considered from a medico-legal viewpoint.

1.4   The remaining two London schools which replied, emphasised departmental and clinical teaching. In one, ethical issues were discussed 'at times' during weekly psychosocial meetings in Medicine and Psychiatry. In Paediatrics, 1 hour weekly of the 8-week course was concerned with ethical issues arising from the rest of the course. Since clinical information relevant to the latter might be provided during the ethics hour, this attracted 90% student attendance, although timetabled for 3.30pm on a Friday afternoon. Every 4 to 6 weeks, the same department held multidisciplinary ethics workshops, in which local community representatives were involved. The final school's philosophy emphasised bedside teaching, but in the pre-clinical course each student had 3 hours of small-group discussion on ethical issues related to human sexuality and reproduction. Ethical topics were included also in General Practice seminars, and consent and confidentiality discussed in Forensic Medicine lectures. A major contribution was made by the Professor of Surgery, who gave an introductory lecture on ethics on the first day of the clinical course and included 2 or 3 1-hour ethics tutorials in the surgical unit firm through which every student passed. This professor's own view was that ethical issues were involved in about half of the 40 hours clinical tuition which each student received from him.

Replies from schools in the rest of England and Northern Ireland

2.1 One of the English Provincial schools described medical ethics as 'a thread woven into the fabric of the course'. While the metaphor was peculiar to this school, the sentiment was echoed elsewhere. In the pre-clinical teaching of this and one other school, for example, ethics was integrated with courses which introduced students to clinical realities from the outset, while in a third, it was integrated with a more community-oriented pre-clinical course.

2.2 In terms of the pre-clinical timetable, the first school mentioned three occasions when ethical issues were raised: first, a formal lecture discussing the problems of clinical decision-making; second, a course of four lectures, entitled 'Medicine and the Medical Student', on drug abuse, alcohol abuse, venereal disease and contraception; and third, opportunities within a) the basic medical sciences course, to discuss the ethics of experiments on man, and b) the community health course, to discuss attitudes, communication and the ethics of resource allocation. The second school, by contrast, laid greater emphasis on its small tutorial groups, led by GPs, which provided a regular opportunity to discuss ethical problems arising at different points in the human life-cycle or in relation to particular patients with whom students had contact. In addition, this school included: a) a 1-hour formal lecture on professional ethics; and b) a 2-hour discussion introduced by a video illustrating problems in the management of a congenitally malformed neonate. The third school also reported provision for small group discussion of ethical issues as they arose in the pre-clinical course, together with 6 hours specifically set aside for seminars on ethical issues. In each of these schools, a variety of pre-clinical and clinical departments were involved in these ethics sessions.

2.3 Reporting on ethics teaching in the clinical years, these three schools all mentioned the provision of seminars or discussions on relevant problem areas, by such departments as Psychiatry, Paediatrics, Obstetrics, Health Care of the Elderly, Medicine, Surgery and Community Medicine. Two of these schools mentioned also a final-year Forensic Medicine or medico-legal lecture course: one of these comprised 6 lectures covering 'consent, confidentiality, "ownership" of records, the Human Tissues Act and the GMC'; in the other, of 8 hours, the topics covered were listed as 'legal system, coroner's administration, medical ethics, sudden death, identification, criminal wounding, exposure and negligence, criminal abortion'.

2.4 The amount of ethics teaching reported by the other medical schools in the English Provinces and Northern Ireland varied considerably. One school, for example, gave 'no particular encouragement' to informal departmental discussion of medical ethics, and mentioned only its fourth-year Forensic Medicine formal lectures, in which 'instruction is given in legal obligations to patients, to NHS, to coroners etc.'. But even this school intended, in the following year, to invite 'some well known speakers to give a lecture on their topic and to meet interested students for discussion informally afterwards', albeit on an extra-curricular basis. In contrast to this, another school not only had arranged a twice-yearly series of 8 lunchtime seminars on medical ethics, but, in its Dean's view, ethical issues were raised regularly in its clinical teaching, which was done in small groups based on clinical teams or a supervisor system. This school, in addition, offered as a pre-clinical option a course specifically on law and ethics.

2.5 In the seven remaining English schools which replied, ethics was most commonly reported to be taught in: a) introductory clinical courses; b) Forensic Medicine course; and c) departmental teaching. Three schools mentioned one or two lectures in their introduction to clinical studies: in the first, the lecture was 'given jointly by a Professor of Medicine, a general practitioner and a consultant in another specialty'; the second had a 1-hour lecture on medical ethics and a ¾-hour lecture on medico-legal issues; the third stated the lecture's objective as 'to provide an awareness of medical ethics and doctor/patient relationships'. In a fourth school, similar topics were discussed in two lectures (in all, of 2½ hours) on 'responsibilities of the medical profession' and 'ethical principles and practice', but as part of the Community Medicine course. A fifth school mentioned '1 hour in the final clinical years'.

2.6 The first three schools mentioned in the previous paragraph each reported some ethics teaching in Forensic Medicine. The first and second each had a 1-hour lecture, the third, a course of 5 lectures: various topics covered included the GMC, negligence, certification and confidentiality. The third school mentioned also 'a 3-hour session on Ethics using video exercises and small group discussion' during its fourth year. Departmental ethics teaching was reported by each of these seven schools: the departments most involved were Medicine, Surgery, Psychiatry, Obstetrics and Gynaecology, Paediatrics, Community Medicine and General Practice or Primary Medical Care. One school reported that 'all major departments except Pathology claim to encourage informal discussion, especially during clinical teaching'. Four of the schools however were more specific: one reported 'involvement by Oncologists and Transplant Team in their teaching blocks'; and a second wrote of two final year lecture/discussions on care of the dying, arranged by a hospice physician. In a third school, there were 10 to 12 hours of lectures in the third and final years, involving the Departments of Psychiatry, Medicine and General Practice. In a fourth, there was a 10-hour course in the fourth year on Ethics and Legal Medicine, which mostly took the form of discussions and involved not only medical staff, but also others 'from a variety of University departments'. This course was held from 3 pm to 5 pm on Friday afternoons and was voluntary. An additional form of teaching was reported by the first school mentioned in 2.5 above. In this school, ethical issues were regularly raised in a weekly tutorial (for which a student prepared a quarter of an hour introduction and was encouraged to do background reading) held during attachment to one of the two surgical firms through which students passed.

Replies from schools in Scotland

3.1   Ethics teaching has been expanded in each of the four Scottish medical schools with clinical as well as pre-clinical curricula. Pre-clinical teaching is undertaken in the Faculty of Science of a fifth Scottish University, but no ethics teaching is included, this being left to the students' clinical schools subsequently. Since one of the Scottish schools elected to reply by departments, and since ethics teaching in the others varies, each is described in turn.

3.2   In the first school, traditionally, 'obvious ethical issues as they arise in patient care' were discussed 'in most clinical specialities', and there was teaching in Community Medicine about prevention, resource priorities and ethical aspects of the doctor-patient relationship (the last discussed also in General Practice). There was also a 1-hour tutorial on Ethical Issues in Reproduction in the fourth-year Obstetrics block. After 1983, four further components were added. The first was a series of four 1½-hour seminars, organised by the Community Medicine Department for first-year students. The seminars included an audio-visual presentation followed by group discussion with fifth-year students assisting as tutors: logistic difficulties however, led to these seminars being temporarily suspended in the year following their introduction. The other three components were: 3 hours of seminars on Ethics in Medicine in second-year Behavourial Science; and case conferences of 1 hour in fourth-year Child Health and of 2 to 6 hours in fifth year Medicine.

3.3   In the second school, a new course was introduced in the fourth year. Regarded 'as supplementing teaching in other courses (e.g. Forensic Medicine, Clinical Teaching)', this course comprises a 1-hour whole-class lecture on 'Moral Argument: An Introduction to Medical Ethics', followed by a 1-hour whole-class question and answer session. The class is then divided into groups of 20 students, each of which has 6 case-based sessions, from 4 pm to 5 pm on designated days, discussing Sanctity of Life, Problems of Confidentiality, Informed Consent, Ethics in Research, Finite Resources and Truth Telling. The introductory lecture is provided by the University Department of Philosophy, while the discussion sessions are normally led by a member of that department and a clinician.

3.4   A not dissimilar scheme has been developed by the third Scottish school. This takes place over 5 weeks in third-year Medicine, each session lasting from 2 pm to 4 pm. In the first week there is a whole-class introductory session with the Professor of Philosophy and a medical professor, who also lead the concluding session in week 5. In weeks 2 to 4, the class is divided so that each student may attend 6 small-group 2-hour sessions on The Role of the Doctor, Ethical Issues in Screening, Negligence and Complaints, Consent, Wise Use of Resources in Hospital, and Dilemmas of High Technology Medicine. In addition to this course and to clinical teaching, the curriculum of this school also includes a 20-lecture Medical Jurisprudence course in its fourth year. Earlier, in the second year, the Environment, Behaviour and Health course includes a lecture and seminars from the Professor of Philosophy on 'Introducing Moral Arguments'.

3.5   The fourth Scottish school distributed the Working Party's questionnaire to its departments, many of which replied. In addition to lectures in Forensic Medicine, timetabled hours of ethics teaching were reported by

Community Medicine, Geriatric Medicine and Obstetrics. The 18 other departments which replied, however, all expressed some interest in the subject and in almost all cases indicated how it was involved in their teaching.

3.6   Replies from these 18 departments illustrated the range and variety of this teaching. **Clinical Chemistry**, for example, saw itself as trying 'to inculcate a responsible and ethically correct attitude to the performance of laboratory tests for the diagnosis and management of illness': it did this by stressing 'the importance of having a reason for investigating patients' and by discouraging 'excessive use and misuse of laboratory investigations'. **Clinical Pharmacology**, similarly, 'put material into the course which could rightly be described as the use and abuse of drugs'; while **Bacteriology** encouraged informal discussion 'on an *ad hoc* basis in tutorials when ethical issues arise, e.g. in relation to aspects of rubella, hepatitis B, AIDS, sexually transmissible diseases, etc.'.

3.7   Some of these subjects, presumably, were among those 'issues, controversial or not', about which **Genito-Urinary Medicine** encouraged 'open discussion' in its one-to-one clinical teaching. **Anaesthetics**, by contrast, regretted that with its 'obvious' interest in intensive care, it was 'able to offer only the most superficial mention of ethical considerations' because of 'the existing constraints of the undergraduate curriculum'. A similar regret was expressed by **Surgery/Urology**: its major ethical interest in renal transplantation was discussed fully in departmental meetings with the few elective students who attended these; but the curriculum otherwise allowed only 30 minutes in Phase II 'to discuss the whole subject of transplantation'. (But see 3.12 below.)

3.8   Among the issues discussed by other clinical departments, **ENT**, for example, mentioned those related to 'the treatment of head and neck cancer and the patient's role in deciding his treatment'; while **Surgical Neurology** took 'care to discuss with all students the concepts of brain death and the significance of various degrees of neurological disability', as well as 'issues of which patients should be treated and which not'. In **Respiratory Medicine**, ethical issues were 'discussed as appropriate in clinical teaching', examples being 'What to tell patients with lung cancer. How to get informed consent to use cytotoxic chemotherapy in cancer'. **Ophthalmology** saw 'ethical overtones in almost everything', specifically mentioning the cost-benefit of screening, X-rays and other matters. **Orthopaedic Surgery**, on the other hand, referred to general ethical principles, including that of double effect, and those concerned with justifying surgery to save life or relieve pain. **Medical Radiology** discussed ethical issues 'in the context of choice and limited resources'.

3.9   Some major clinical Departments were less specific. **Clinical Surgery** stated that 'ethical aspects of treatment options are frequently discussed as part of our teaching'; and **Psychiatry** reported that in its 'tutorials and discussions about patients, ethical issues constantly intrude owing to the nature of the human problems encountered'. For seven years, Psychiatry had assigned two meetings annually of each of its small tutorial groups to discussion in which the teaching psychiatrist was accompanied by a visitor from the University Philosophy or Divinity departments. Most of the consultant psychiatrists however, 'did not feel that these sessions were a great success', and they had 'simply petered out'. It was now felt that 'the best way to instil our students with a belief that they should constantly be considering medical ethics' was 'through apprenticeship and tutorial discussion about human problems'.

3.10 **General Practice** also reported in general terms. 'Many of the consultations seen by our students contain ethical problems which form the basis of further discussion either at the time of the consulting session or later in small groups'. During the seven weeks spent in **Paediatrics**, that department reported, 'the subject of ethics is often discussed in clinical situations: malformed infants, very low birth weight infants, terminally ill children, illegitimate children, brain-dead children, grossly handicapped children. How officiously should we strive to keep alive? When should treatment stop?'

3.11 Neither of the school's two Departments of **Medicine** had timetabled provision for ethics teaching. But one stated that all teaching staff were provided with 'objectives which include a note on "attitudes"'. Issues 'discussed in Medicine, relating to ethics' were 'Allocation of scarce resources, Doctor/patient relationships including confidentiality, Ethics of clinical research, Over-investigation, Over-treatment, Termination of treatment e.g. kidney dialysis, Euthanasia'. In the other Medicine department, ward rounds 'held every morning from 8.30 to 9.15 frequently involve discussions with students on ethical issues'. This department, with Ophthalmology, had sponsored a series of 8 lectures on 'Logic in Medicine'. The course, held at 5.15 pm on Tuesdays, included lectures by philosophers on ethics and on formal logic, as well as clinicians on diagnostic logic. It was 'very badly attended' however by the Phase II students at whom it was aimed.

3.12 Timetabled periods during the clinical course at this school included lectures traditionally undertaken by **Forensic Medicine**. The subjects covered included: 'Medical etiquette, The General Medical Council, Medical negligence, Medicolegal aspects of ventilator death and organ transplantation, Deaths associated with operation and/or anaesthesia, Consent to treatment and experimentation'. For a number of years, the Forensic Medicine Department and the Faculty of Law had also organised, for the latter's students, a highly successful Medical Jurisprudence course.

3.13 In the first year of the pre-clinical course, **Community Medicine** organised a 2-hour whole-class session on Ethics. This began with a short general introduction to ethics by a philosopher or theologian, followed by three case presentations by clinicians and general practitioners, with a nurse commenting and leading to general discussion in each case. In the same year, over two terms, students undertook group projects, a number of which (related to terminal care, emergency departments, abortion and psychiatric treatment) involved discussion of ethical issues with philosophers as well as some contact with patients. Some teaching in the second year also raised ethical questions about resource allocation and other matters related to the NHS.

3.14 Ethics teaching in **Obstetrics and Gynaecology** took place in Phase II and Phase III. In the former, a 3-week block was so organised that each student had at least one morning devoted to ethical problems in reproductive medicine. The format was that one, two or three case histories were presented to a class of about 40 students, with input from wide variety of professionals and relevant lay groups. To include all students in the year, the sessions were held on four consecutive mornings. In Phase III, a 1-hour tutorial was set aside for discussion of ethical problems. The tutorial was introduced by a student with a case presentation illustrating ethical issues arising from his or her attachment to Obstetrics and Gynaecology wards, and the discussion was led by a representative of the local Medical Group. These tutorials were available only to those students attached to the main teaching hospital.

3.15 Within the timetabled formal teaching in **Geriatric Medicine** was included a whole morning visit to the local hospice, when the students received a talk from its Director, saw patients and talked to staff. Problems of terminal care, pain relief and what to tell patients and relatives were all discussed in an informal fashion with students in groups of about 16. On a further occasion, at the end of a 3-week clinical clerkship, students had a day in the department when they were required to present a case which had caught their attention. A very high proportion of these cases presented ethical problems and were discussed in groups of about 16 students, in the presence of one or more members of staff, the Professor of Forensic Medicine, or a representative of the local Medical Group. One of the Educational Objectives of the Geriatric Medicine course was 'The importance of protection of the liberty of the individual so that the elderly may retain maximum choice and control over their own life styles and the manner in which they face dying'. Every student was given a copy of the objectives. Ethical considerations frequently raised in relation to individual patients, the department stated, were mostly about patients' rights, but also about 'when to treat or investigate'. The importance of seeking advice from other health professionals (especially the nursing profession) was stressed, as was the need to discuss these matters with members of the patient's family.

APPENDIX TWO

Teaching medical ethics: the contribution of philosophy, moral theology and law

Papers by Dr Jonathan Glover, Professor Keith Ward, Fr Brendan Callaghan SJ, and Professor Gerald Dworkin

PHILOSOPHY
Jonathan Glover

In our discussions in the working party, there has been a fair amount of agreement that "medical ethics" has at least two components worth considering separately:

1. The formal or informal code of practice that guides decisions about moral issues arising in medicine.

2. The techniques of critical thinking about morality. These are likely to be drawn upon where there is a conflict between different principles embodied in the code of practice, or where principles previously accepted start to be questioned.

There seems to be some consensus among us that the teaching of medical ethics should include both these aspects. The contribution of philosophy is to the second component. Philosophy has, of course, no monopoly on the techniques of critical thinking, and its contribution as it will be described here has considerable overlap with that of moral theology and of legal thinking.

When moral philosophy is mentioned in a medical context, some doctors hope (or, more often fear) that the aim is to come up with some set of principles which will give the right answer when applied to any medico-moral problem. Or, less ambitiously, the aim is thought to be, if not right answers, at least consensus. I shall give reasons for thinking both these aims misguided. Philosophy at its best succeeds in the more modest aim of helping people to think more clearly about the issues and so to understand them better. This aim, though more modest, is not a minor one.

(Philosophy "at its best" achieves this. Like any discipline, philosophy has its share of the mediocre and the incompetent. The equivalent of iatrogenic disease is when philosophers leave people more muddled or dogmatic than they were before.)

1. Moral argument

The contribution of philosophy to medical ethics centres around examining the reasons people give for ethical views. It is about moral argument. But this presupposes that there is room for argument about morality. That there is room for argument is denied by some widely held views.

On one view, morality is a body of doctrine whose truth is immediately apparent. According to one version, we know what is right by a kind of infallible inner intuition. Another version appeals to authority: we can settle moral issues by appealing to the commands of God or the teachings of a church. If we follow either of these lines of thought, the role of argument is either non-existent or is limited to questions about interpreting the authority.

These approaches to ethics have well known difficulties. The appeal to intuitive moral knowledge has the problem of marking it off from mere gut reactions. And appeals to authority have the problem of supporting the claim that a particular church or individual has a hot line to God.

At the other extreme is a view of ethics perhaps more influential in our society. On this view, moral beliefs are a matter of subjective opinion about which argument is pointless. Just as it is silly to try to argue someone out of a preference for tea over coffee, so it is thought to be silly to try to argue someone out of their attitude to abortion. On this approach, just as much as on the other one, moral argument has no role.

There are reasons for rejecting this denial of the possibility of argument. It is possible to accept that there may be no objective moral truths, without having to agree that argument is impossible. A great deal of the argument that is possible consists in asking people to describe, more fully than they are used to doing, their beliefs and their reasons for holding them, and then pressing them about consistency. Supporters of abortion may be asked if they are against infanticide, and if so on what principle they draw the line. Opponents of abortion may be asked for their reasons. If they say that taking human life is always wrong, they may be asked if they are absolute pacifists. If not, something has to give. They must change their mind about pacifism, or else abandon or modify their principle that taking human life is always wrong.

These are crude and simple examples, but they bring out something of both the force and limitations of moral argument. Anyone sufficiently rational to be disturbed by inconsistency can be pushed in the direction of elaborating and perhaps modifying their views. So moral argument is not pointless. But it is in an important way limited. Someone may have to change his views about either pacifism or about the universal wrongness of taking human life. But he has a choice. Nothing forces him to modify one rather than the other. And different people will often choose differently. Argument can be a powerful tool, but an opponent determined to hang on to a position can do so by making the appropriate choices about what to give up when inconsistencies are exposed.

The choices we make depend a lot on our intuitive responses to particular cases. Systems of moral belief are "tested" by the intuitive acceptability or unacceptability of what they commit us to. If I come across some particularly repulsive animal experiment, I may decide that I am morally opposed to all vivisection. But when I think about the benefits of medical research, and think of my intuitive response to a child dying of a disease, I have a countervailing response which may make me change this view. There is an interplay between general principles and intuitive responses which to some extent resembles the interplay between theory and observation in science. But ethics is not science, and it is implausible to claim that we are dealing with objective truths. For this reason there is room for ultimate and unresolvable disagreement between people. But the point where argument breaks down does not come nearly as soon as is often thought, and a great deal can be learnt on the way there.

2. Moral argument in medicine

Philosophical examination of moral argument in a medical context would fall into three broad areas:

(a) EXAMINING REASONS GIVEN FOR A MORAL VIEW.

Perhaps the reason for a view is that the doctor-patient relationship requires the doctor to do, or to refrain from doing, something. At this point, questions can be asked about how the requirements of this relationship are determined. To what extent do the interests of the patient over-ride, say, the

52

interests of other members of his or her family? Does it require absolute confidentiality? Even if the diagnosis is AIDS?

Or the reason given for a decision taken about a severely handicapped baby may be that "not striving to keep alive" is quite different from euthanasia. Questions again can be asked about how the distinction is drawn and about the reasons for thinking it morally significant. Is withholding nourishment "killing" or "letting die"? And why should the decision be judged so differently according to which of these labels applies?

The examination of these reasons will involve making explicit the underlying principles they rest on, and then testing them for consistency, perhaps by seeing how the same principles stand up in quite different contexts.

(b)   CLARIFICATION OF THE CONCEPTS.

Often the expression of a moral belief will use concepts which are unclear, in ways that may blur the thinking behind a decision. Examples are "informed consent", "acceptable risk", "person" (as used in the abortion debate), and "mental illness". Exposure to the published discussions of these problematic concepts heightens awareness of the existence of alternative criteria, (e.g. for what counts as being "informed") and of the different principles that might justify adopting one set of criteria rather than another. But, more important than knowledge of problems about a particular set of concepts is a heightened awareness of such conceptual issues and the development of an analytical style of thinking about them.

(c)   DISCUSSION OF THE FOUNDATIONS OF A MORAL SYSTEM.

As someone's moral beliefs, under pressure of requests for reasons, start to be spelt out in a systematic way, certain basic elements often stand out more clearly. The system may centre around some absolute prohibitions, perhaps forbidding intentional killing, or treating people as means rather than ends in themselves. Or the system may be utilitarian, or some other version of a consequence-based approach, so that the question of, say, lying to patients is seen in terms of its beneficial or harmful outcome. Or it may stress respect for autonomy, or more generally respecting the rights people are held to have.

As the basic elements emerge, more general problems of justification arise. For instance, a system based on respecting rights raises the problem of how we decide what rights people have, and what to do when they conflict. In the abortion debate, the right to life of the unborn child is opposed to the woman's right to choose. How are we to decide which, if either, of these supposed rights is genuine? If both are, on what grounds does one take priority? Problems of similar seriousness arise for the other theories, and a great deal of ingenuity has gone into both attacking and defending the different approaches. Studying this does not lead to the development of an impregnable moral system. But it is hard to believe in the intelligence of anyone who studies this work and emerges with all his or her original views unmodified.

3.   What should be the intended benefits for doctors and patients?

It would be nice to be able to claim that these theoretical studies would ensure that the students, on becoming doctors, would take the "right" decisions in morally problematic cases. But such a claim would require critical thinking to be capable of decisively establishing ethical truths, which the students could be taught to recognize. But if the account given here is correct, more modest claims have to be made. Students can be pushed towards consistency, but because there can be more than one consistent moral system, they may well not end up with a consensus.

The case for theoretical ethics has to be made without implying that the students will discover ethical truths. The case partly rests on the claim that these studies will sometimes lead to different decisions from those that would otherwise have been taken, and that these decisions are in some sense "better". But there is also a case which is independent of any change in the decisions doctors make. I will start with this second case.

The quality of a decision can vary without its outcome being different. In medicine, the results of a well conducted trial may be misleading. And some old wives' tale may contain medical truth. But we may still think more highly of a doctor who goes by the evidence rather than by what his grandfather told him. In the same way, other things equal, I would prefer the decision about whether or not to keep me alive to be taken by someone who had thought systematically and clearly about the kinds of reasons that could be given, rather than by someone who went by what the consultant told him when he was a student. They might come to the same decision, but the difference in the quality of thinking behind it is not trivial.

I think I would not be alone among patients in preferring one approach to the other. But it is possible that some medical students would feel that they themselves had gained from exposure to the kind of critical thinking described. They might not end up thinking they were taking more "right" decisions. But they might value having more idea of what is going on in moral thinking, and having more awareness of the kind of thinking behind moral views other than their own. Part of the case for theoretical ethics rests on the value of greater intellectual awareness. This part of the case is parallel to the case for teaching scientific method rather than teaching medicine merely by rote learning. It is part of a more general view that doctors, like other people, gain from a humane education in their subject rather than from a narrow technician's training.

Perhaps more surprisingly, another part of the case rests on an extension of understanding and sympathy, which comes from seeing that those you disagree with are neither wicked nor stupid. (Though their position of course has problems in the same way yours does.)

These considerations are independent of critical ethics having any detectable impact on the decisions that doctors take. But it must be admitted that, with many other claims on time and resources, if these studies had virtually **no** influence on decisions, the case for them might not be overwhelming.

There is an even gloomier thought than that no difference would be made: perhaps decisions would be changed, but could this be for the worse? If I could choose to place life and death decisions about myself in the hands either of a group of doctors or a group of philosophers, I should without hesitation choose the doctors. But despite this, the view that doctors might on the whole take better decisions after exposure to ethics can be defended. How is this possible?

Doctors and philosophers have different strengths. Good doctors develop a sensitivity to the human consequences of different courses of action, an intuitive feel for the relative weight of different factors, which they may not always be good at articulating in discussion. (Watching doctors facing critics on Ian Kennedy's television programmes, it often seemed that they had more feel than their critics for what would matter to patients, but the critics ran rings round them in argument. I would choose Ian Kennedy as my lawyer but some of his victims as my doctor.) Good philosophers reason well but often do not have much feel for the human aspects of these decisions. In philosophy, reputations are gained for cleverness and ingenuity rather than for humanity. So some highly able philosophical writings on ethics have a remoteness from human reality that makes it better for them not to be taken as guides.

The hope I have, perhaps a bit optimistic, but perhaps not quite unrealistic, is that, through linking medicine and ethics, the virtues of the two approaches might more often be fused. The intuitive sensitivity of doctors might combine with a more analytial approach to underlying principles to produce something nearer the ideal decision maker than the average doctor or philosopher is now. (A beneficial side effect, if philosophers were involved in teaching, might be an improvement in their feel for the human side of the decisions, with their theoretical work being correspondingly enriched.) But the practical effect on doctors' decisions which could be expected is that they would less often be based on reasoning that is simple-minded or confused. Even if there are no objectively true answers to be discovered to these moral dilemmas, it is not absurd to hope that patients might benefit more from decisions taken by doctors with a clearer grasp of the complex issues involved.

4. How should critical ethics fit into a medical course?

(a) SMALL GROUPS:

Ethics of the kind described here is better taught by discussion than by lectures. The aim is to get students to state their own approaches and to learn to think out the implications and problems. This suggests teaching in small groups. Large groups make it hard to follow an argument through, as well as inhibiting people from offering opinions.

(b) START WITH CASES, NOT THEORY.

This is the only way it will come alive.

(c) SHOULD THERE BE EXAMINATIONS?

The case for examinations is that topics that do not count towards some exam may not be taken seriously. But the danger of having exams is that ethics becomes just one more thing to learn up, and this might not be conducive to the kind of thought we would hope to encourage. On balance I rather hope we do not go for exams.

(d) WHERE IN THE COURSE?

The problems will probably only seem worth studying when they have started to arise in the students' experience. This suggests not starting too early in the course. And, if there are not going to be exams, it should probably not be continued in the run-up to their exams in other subjects. Ideally, ethics would not be hived off in a completely separate course on its own. Making the ethical problems of each specialism part of that course rather than part of an ethics course will keep the ethical issues more real, as well as fitting the policy of making the teaching case based. It also goes with the desirability of:

(e) INTER-DISCIPLINARY TEACHING

The teaching should not just be by philosophers, theologians, etc, any more than just by obstetricians, etc. A problem is that, to start with, there may not be many people, medical or philosophical, who will be confident about teaching in this area. But that is often a problem about new courses, which often teach the teachers as much as the students. Doctors and philosophers will pick up some of the relevant bits of each others' subjects as they teach with each other.

MORAL THEOLOGY 1
Keith Ward

As a theologian, I have little to add to Jonathan Glover's admirable paper. I would hope to teach the subject very much in the way he outlines. I have two small comments, and a short addition to make.

First, I do find the second paragraph of 'moral argument' over-drawn. I know few people who really appeal to infallible inner intuition; and fewer who appeal to God's commands or church teaching as settling moral issues. On the latter point, the interesting issue is how moral decisions are to be derived either from sacred texts or within church institutions; and there are lots of fascinating intellectual moves to explore in those regions. These are too much like 'straw men' for my liking; but perhaps they only need muting a little. There are major problems about the role of authority in ethics which this paragraph tends simply to ignore, but which are deserving of serious treatment, in my view.

Second, at the end of 'moral argument', I do not think it implausible to claim that we are dealing with objective truths. Again, this is precisely one problem I would hope to be able to explore in a moral theology course, at much greater length.

Now for the addition. What would a theologian add to the philosophers' account? Firstly, a factual account of the way various religious traditions have approached issues in medical ethics — the role of authority and different styles of authoritative guidance; and attention to the diversity of responses even within apparently monolithic religious traditions. It is vital that these accounts are not dogmatic or over-simple (e.g. 'The Church says', without seeing why, after what processes of arguments, and exactly when and by whom).

Secondly, an appreciation of different basic attitudes which religions have — which would introduce the question of how very basic beliefs about human nature and destiny affect moral decisions, and how certain sorts of principles tend to get selected as basic elements in a moral scheme.

It could be that some overt attention to these matters would enable the student to see that it is not just a matter of selecting some moral principles and pursuing their consequences; but that fundamental views of the nature of human life may give rise to diverse moral outlooks. Thus ethics could be located within a wider web of beliefs, which might affect one's view of what ethics is.

I am, however, quite clear that what Jonathan Glover outlines would be the major component of any properly reflective approach to problems of medical ethics.

MORAL THEOLOGY 2
Brendan Callaghan SJ

Moral theology and the teaching of medical ethics

That moral theology has a contribution to make to medical ethics teaching may not be self-evident, especially if moral theology is seen as giving rise to moral statements relying on extrinsic authority rather than inherent rationality and argument. Clearly, such statements might appropriately be seen as of importance for those only who accept the authority cited, and of little significance for others. However, moral theology as such, (as distinct from moral exhortation and from moralising), has a different self-understanding which may serve to focus its relevance for medical ethics teaching. This self-understanding may be illustrated by a quotation from a statement produced by the Liaison Committee of the British Council of Churches and the Roman Catholic Church in England and Wales:

> All the BCC member Churches and the Roman Catholic Church agree that Christian moral reflection must be based on scripture, on the tradition of the Church, on the moral experience of individual believers, and on the results of relevant empirical enquiry — all worked upon by reason — even though different Churches may give differing emphasis to each of these resources.

From my own point of view, it would seem to be the moral insights of various and varied 'communities of common belief', articulated and developed over time within the context of a more or less agreed understanding of human nature, that form one distinctive contribution of moral theology. The ways in which these insights, and the procedures by which they have been developed, themselves in turn form material for further reflection, is a point picked up by Professor Ward: I would wish here to draw attention to the appropriateness of recognising (if not going so far as to explore) the moral insights and traditions within which many individuals operate and which form a major part of the cultural context of **all** our moral education, discussion and decision making.

Teaching medical ethics in a non-medical context

For a small number of years, I have been teaching medical ethics in a particular academic setting, namely the Christian Ethics course preparing undergraduate students for the appropriate paper of the London BD, and providing postgraduate students in Pastoral Theology with an introduction to the field. The undergraduate students feel the need to acquire appropriately refined skills enabling them to deal with questions posed by the University examiners, whilst the postgraduate students, (typically on sabbatical from a wide variety of pastoral posts), are looking for ways of articulating their own attempts to make sense of moral dilemmas. This varied constituency, deliberately taught as one group in order to expose each component to the preoccupations and emphases of the other, has benefitted from a case-based approach to introductory teaching in medical ethics.

Each class has focused on a particular area of concern, illustrated by short narrative case-stories, which are explained briefly and amplified where necessary before the class is divided into small groups and asked to arrive at the practical decisions required by each of the stories used. The groups are asked to explore, or at least to note for future exploration, the arguments which emerge in these discussions, and it is these arguments rather than the actual decisions which form the basis for the third part of the teaching time, in which a general discussion is held, situating the points made in the groups within the context of moral theological discussion. Finally, a summary of the issues raised and the various ways in which they have been dealt with is made available in duplicated form together with an introductory booklist.

The method outlined above which requires (but does not always receive) a very careful control of the time available, provides a mechanism by which undergraduate students who may not have given any consideration to the questions raised become engaged in the discussion of the 'real life' problems presented, whilst the more senior students have an opportunity to explore, in a more structured and reflective way, dilemmas of which they are aware to various degrees. The students are provided with an introduction to, rather than a methodical treatment of the ways in which the topics raised have been dealt with by the Christian tradition.

LAW
Gerald Dworkin

Teaching medical ethics: the contribution of law

I have been giving a course on "law and medicine" to **law students** for several years; and I have also participated frequently in medico/legal/ethical discussions with medical students, as well as with other medical personnel. My experience suggests that there are no major differences between these groups in the context of much of the subject matter which can be covered or in the approach to the subject matter.

The law and ethics of medical practice are intricately interrelated. Until recently major medical ethical problems rarely came before the courts in the United Kingdom. The law lurked awkwardly in the background and provided few specific answers to ethical dilemmas. That situation is changing rapidly and ethical dilemmas are being presented to the courts for legal resolution, although often not successfully. Important recent cases which come to mind relate to the amount of information which patients should be given (the *Sidaway* case, 1985); the legality of prescribing contraceptives to teenage girls (the *Gillick* case, 1985); the treatment of handicapped new born infants (the *Dr. Arthur* and *Baby Alexandra* cases). The keen public interest in medical ethics has also been responsible for emergency legislation (*The Surrogacy Arrangements Act* 1985).

Students undertaking a course on medical ethics should have some, albeit limited, legal knowledge. They should be aware of some of the basic legal rules which affect their actions as medical practitioners. Perhaps, more important, they should be made aware that, either because of the normative nature of some legal principles ("was the doctor acting in accordance with acceptable medical standards?"), or because of the curious penumbra of uncertainty which surrounds so much of our law, there are few clear and simple legal answers to the moral problems; and that often a court's assessment of the law may be influenced directly or indirectly by its perceptions of the moral issues involved.

There are several American case books on Law and Medicine for law students. In some of these the emphasis on practical legal issues (for example, detailed analysis of the medical malpractice action) would be inappropriate for a medical ethics course for medical students. Most of these books, however, contain material which would be essential for such courses.

For example:

1. **The relationship between doctor and patient**

    1.1 **Consent to treatment — the role of doctor and patient.** The *Sidaway* and related cases would provide excellent case study material for exploring the relevant issues:

    e.g. autonomy vs. paternalism;
          how much information;

what can, or should, be withheld;
the role of consent forms.

1.2 **Accountability**
— **the nature and role of the "medical malpractice" action:**
establishing the standard of care;
the range of duties;
problems of obtaining and giving evidence;
the value, if any, of such actions;
the role of defence organisations;
alternatives to negligence actions;

(cases such as *Whitehouse v. Jordan* would be appropriate as a case-study bringing out many important issues).

— the role of the **Health Service Commissioner**
— Family Practitioner Committees etc.
— the **General Medical Council** — its jurisdiction and powers; how successful is it in coping with the range of ethical issues that could come before it?

1.3 **Confidentiality**
e.g. The right of access to records;
the obligation of confidence and the exceptions thereto.

2. **Birth and the beginning of life**

2.1 **Avoiding birth:**
— contraception
— abortion
— sterilisation

2.2 **Facilitating birth:**
— artificial conception
— genetic counselling

3. **Death and dying**

3.1 **Definition of death** — the role of the law

3.2 **Facilitating death;**
— withholding assistance
— withdrawing treatment
— resuscitation

4. **"Extraordinary" medical "treatment"**

e.g. transplantation

5. **Clinical research**

Whilst it may be that "the law" should be an adjunct to the analysis of medical ethics, it is difficult to keep it out of most of the areas of medical ethics which would come within a course for medical students. Properly planned and taught, however, courses incorporating relevant legal issues would add to their interest and value.